Truly Mindful Coloring

~ Stay Calm, Reduce Stress, & Self-Express ~

Terry Marks-Tarlow, PhD

foreword by Daniel J. Siegel, MD

Published by
PESI Publishing & Media
PESI, Inc
3839 White Ave
Eau Claire, WI 54703

Cover: Al Postlewaite
Editing: Marietta Whittlesey
Layout: Bookmasters & Al Postlewaite

ISBN: 9781683730316

Printed in the United States of America.

PESI
Publishing
& Media
www.pesipublishing.com

Author and Illustrator
Terry Marks-Tarlow, PhD

I have been a licensed clinical psychologist in private practice in Santa Monica, California, since 1985. I specialize in deep transformation as well as creativity and its blocks. Besides being a psychotherapist and drawing, I have practiced and taught yoga over the past 40 years, and I have been studying ballet and jazz for nearly as long. By maintaining nearly daily dance and yoga practices, I have learned the value of moving meditations.

Before becoming a psychologist, I toyed with the idea of becoming an artist. I have never given up this dream. I continue to draw on a regular basis. In addition to this book, I have written and illustrated four others. Many of the drawings in this book appeared in these books. I write about nonlinear science and the importance of clinical intuition to effective therapy.

In my personal life, I practice being creative partly by taking emotional risks. I jumped fields to write the libretto for an opera, entitled "Cracked Orlando," that opened in 2010 in New York City with a ballet. Out of a deep commitment to the healing role of creativity, I co-founded and continue to curate a yearly art exhibition of psychotherapist art sponsored by the Los Angeles County Psychological Association, entitled "Mirrors of the Mind: The Psychotherapist as Artist." This book emerged partly out of the ongoing inspiration from my fellow psychotherapist artists as well as from my incredibly creative patients. I hope the pages that follow serve to inspire you as well. www.markstarlow.com

Foreword Writer
Daniel J. Siegel, MD

Daniel J. Siegel, M.D., is a graduate of Harvard Medical School and completed his postgraduate medical education at UCLA with training in pediatrics and child, adolescent and adult psychiatry. He is a clinical professor of psychiatry at the UCLA School of Medicine, founding co-director of UCLA's Mindful Awareness Research Center, founding co-investigator at the UCLA Center for Culture, Brain and Development, and executive director of the Mindsight Institute, an educational center devoted to promoting insight, compassion, and empathy in individuals, families, institutions and communities.

Dr. Siegel's psychotherapy practice spans 30 years, and he has published extensively for the professional audience. He serves as the founding editor for the Norton Professional Series on Interpersonal Neurobiology which includes over three dozen textbooks. Dr. Siegel's books include *Mindsight, Pocket Guide to Interpersonal Neurobiology, The Developing Mind*, Second Edition, *The Mindful Therapist, The Mindful Brain, Parenting form the Inside Out* (with Mary Hartzell, M.Ed.), and the three *New York Times* bestsellers: *Brainstorm, The Whole-Brain Child* (with Tina Payne Bryson, Ph.D.), and *No-Drama Discipline* (with Tina Payne Bryson, Ph.D). His latest book is *Mind: A Journey to the Heart of Being Human*. He has been invited to lecture for the King of Thailand, Pope John Paul II, His Holiness the Dalai Lama, Google University, and TEDx. For more information about his educational programs and resources, please visit: www.DrDanSiegel.com

Table of Contents

Acknowledgments

This book would not have been possible without generous contributions of time, energy and photographs plus fabulous feedback from the following: Gitu Bhatia, Shira Brown, Melanie Jackson-Cracchiolo, Peg Cummings, Marlena Elise, Christine Forest, Patricia Greenfield, Sheila Gross, Ping Ho, Beth Jakubanis, Alexandra Katehakis, Pamela McCrory, Dave Menken, Jill Nevins, Lisa Owens, Jahna Perricone, Joanna Poppink, Linda Pushkin-Suffin, Cat Ramos, Toby Salkin, Ericha Hitchcock Scott, Michael Shiffman, Daniel Siegel, Victoria Stevens, Buz Tarlow, Cody Tarlow, and Darby Tarlow. Many thanks to Karsyn Morse, Al Postlewaite, and the wonderful PESI staff for believing in and helping to actualize the potential of this book.

Foreword

We live in a world often filled with words, spending much of our time thinking about things, and taking in the array of auditory and visual stimuli that fill our senses with never-ending input. Imagine taking a big breath, pausing, and finding a way of being that offers a complementary approach to our lives. In your hands you have just such a pathway to a new way of seeing and being: Terry Marks-Tarlow's *Truly Mindful Coloring* is truly wonderful—filled with wonder.

We can imagine that the circuitry of the brain involved in linguistic processing, rational thinking, and even the intake of sensory stimuli are balanced in a helpful way by taking a pause in your life to let words go, release the rational processing that dominates your life, and enables the directionality of living to transition from reception to expression. With these marvelous figures, you can use your hand-eye coordination to lay down whatever color schemes arise in your imagination, giving yourself permission to let impulses and intuitive sensations arise and guide your eyes and your hands.

You may be wondering, isn't such "mind-wandering" just what we are not supposed to be doing for our well-being? Many studies suggest that unintentional scattering of our attention is indeed associated with unhappiness—but this is actually quite different from this scattered mind state. Here you'll *intentionally* be giving yourself permission to enter a playful state. What this means is that you can relax your concern about others' expectations, enabling the spontaneous emergence of whatever arises on the page to unfold without a sense of others directing the outcome. Playfulness is one of the most underdeveloped states in our adult repertoire—yet research affirms that giving yourself time to be playful, to open yourself up to let things emerge for just what they are and not for some designed outcome, is a crucial part of our daily mental diet for a well-nourishing life.

In many ways, the mindful coloring that our guide offers us here is filled with the sense of permission to explore the intricate figures she has masterfully created. We can then enable our sense of color to explode on the page, following a hunch, an intuitive sense, an urge, that then emerges on the page as a wash of color. As the colors emerge, we then can take them in, pause, and just get a sense of what feelings arise within us. As you let your eyes now pass over your choice of a colored pen or pencil, you may find your hand reaches for one you may not have *thought* about using, but you *felt* it in your non-verbal mind, sensing it as an image, a bodily sensation, or perhaps simply the movement of your hand to that color.

Whether you use this for your own mindful explorations, or help guide others in individual, couples or group therapy settings, the invitation is the same: Being mindful involves distinguishing a sensory stream of awareness, an observational one, a conceptual one, and even a large overarching knowing one. These distinctions free the mind to become more integrated as we learn to take these differentiated elements of mental life and link them to each other. An integrated mind is the basis of well-being.

Facilitating this integration, our artist/therapist guide provides brilliantly divided sections that explore some fundamental aspects of our mental lives: Creating Inner Refuge Through Stilling the Mind, Focusing Your Mind into Laser Beam Attention, Cultivating an Open, Receptive Mind, Enhancing Creativity and Play by Making Associations, Fostering a Compassionate Mind to Take Care of Self and Others. The poetic summaries within each of these chapters are themselves works of art, and works of heart. Soak these words of wisdom in, even before you bring color to the magical line drawings that accompany and expand each one. You may find yourself deeply expressing the meaning of the entry, and then reflecting, both in the coloring and later on as images and further reflections, on the layers of significance that these chapters invite us to weave into our own lives.

For anyone on a journey to become more present, these entries and their drawings invite a powerful integration of the four streams of awareness. We take in the sensory fullness of the drawings and let that sit within our being. We soak in the observational stance of what these words invite us to reflect upon, observing, witnessing and even narrating their meaning in our lives. And we have a deep conceptual stream that arises, both from the poetic phrases and the fabulous figures, as we permit a deep sense of knowing to arise. Sensation, observation, conceptualizing, and knowing—these are the differentiated ways of sensing the world that are distinguished and then linked within this wonderful experience.

Truly Mindful Coloring invites us to create a mindful experience as we integrate our minds to create more well-being for ourselves and others. Soak in this experience – its words of wisdom and playful and profound figures – as you dive into the immersion that awaits. The only intentions you need to invite yourself to create are the gifts of time, the gifts of freedom to express and explore, and the gift of letting things simply emerge. Let the presents of these gifts be the presence of mind at the heart of well-being in our individual lives and our collective relationships with each other, and with life itself.

—Daniel J. Siegel, MD

INTRODUCTION
Why be Mindful?

As we move through life, we can either *tune into* our selves—what we are feeling, sensing and doing—or we can *tune out*. When exercising, for example, we can either drift away from our bodies by reviewing what just happened at work or daydreaming about the meal to come. Or, we can stay grounded in our present-centered, body-based experience. The more actively we engage with ongoing perceptions, feelings, and sensations, the more grounded we feel and the more pleasure and presence we can cultivate in life.

Broadly speaking, mindfulness involves tuning into present-centered awareness. Mindfulness is not an activity per se, but instead is a way of living. Just as there are many ways to tune into current experience, there are also multiple understandings of the very concept of mindfulness.

During a given moment, how to tune in mindfully depends upon:

- *Who* we are
- *Where* we are
- *What* activity we engage in
- *What intentions* we set for ourselves

Different places, situations, activities and intentions not only engage different qualities of attention, but also different parts of the brain and different aspects of our brain/mind/body unity. How to pay attention in a mindful way will differ tremendously, depending upon what we are trying to do:

- If sitting quietly in meditation, we need a still mind;
- If studying for a test, we need a focused mind;
- When exploring an unknown place, we need an open mind;
- When trying to solve a problem, we need an associative mind;
- When engaging meaningfully with others, we need a compassionate mind.

It is important to gain the flexibility and adaptability to suit our quality of awareness to the precise conditions in which we find ourselves. To cultivate these various qualities of attention plus learn how to shift fluidly between them is much like exercising the body. We begin by isolating and exercising all of the muscle groups, not just one set. This prepares us to coordinate them all in an integrated fashion, while developing strength, stretch, balance, focus, and grace. So too with the mind. The more we practice each type of awareness, the better we can get at shifting between them and tuning into the fullness of present-centered awareness without resistance, judgment, or cognitive filters. This helps us to gain confidence and relax into our deepest selves.

Each of us has internal habits that remove us from presence of mind. To become more mindful, it helps to become more aware of your own challenges and blocks.

These questions point you in that direction:

- Do you act impulsively, automatically, or without thinking?

- Do you think too much and repetitively, with the same thoughts looping around and around?

- Do you become stuck in the past, either by regretting or ruminating over events?

- Do you rush toward the future, either through excessive planning or worry?

- Do you zone out by disconnecting from your emotions or bodily experience?

- Do you become preoccupied by your internal experience no matter where you are?

- Do you become hypervigilant to the outside world, such that awareness gets riveted or drifts continually outside of yourself?

- Do you focus on other people excessively, by judging or comparing yourself according to their appearance, differences or expectations?

By bringing more awareness to our own mental habits, we can then respond by setting conscious intentions. To set an intention, first take stock of your being and body. Then let the totality of who you are tell you how to focus attention during an upcoming activity. Setting an intention is different from setting a goal. When we set a goal, we direct attention narrowly in order to focus on a result or outcome. When we set an intention, we are more interested in the process. We broaden our attention to open up a wide space of possibilities. Setting intentions is common in yoga. Sometimes we need to pull back and rest. Sometimes we need to cultivate inner fire and engage with ambition. Sometimes we need to stay focused on the breath. Other times we wish to cultivate inner peace and equanimity. As you move through the pages in this book, try setting an intention each time you sit down to draw.

INTENTION OF THIS BOOK

Truly Mindful Coloring is designed to foster different qualities of awareness while offering varied opportunities to engage in mindful drawing. The book is divided into five chapters. Each one corresponds to a different quality of attention. Each chapter also contains a set of 12 drawings with content relevant to that quality of mind. Every chapter begins with targeted education surrounding the nature and importance of that quality of attention.

Here are the five chapters:

- Creating Inner Refuge Through Stilling the Mind
- Focusing Your Mind into Laser Beam Attention
- Cultivating an Open, Receptive Mind
- Enhancing Creativity and Play by Making Associations
- Fostering a Compassionate Mind to Take Care of Self and Others

By self-reflecting upon different feelings, internal truths, and needs as you draw, you can practice mindfulness and ensure that you're not simply tuning out, disengaging, or operating on automatic. By drawing mindfully for prolonged periods of time, you can get into flow states that will enhance your ability to extend mindful awareness into all of your activities during everyday life.

CULTIVATE YOUR CREATIVITY!

Some artists and art therapists object to coloring books, under the presumption that they crimp rather than encourage creativity. These folks have a good point, as lots of tiny spaces greatly narrows attention and leaves little room for creative decisions other than color choice. Of course, color choice is itself a creative act, especially when we deviate from how things appear in real life. But adult coloring books also hold great potential for other sorts of creativity as well.

When producing these pages, I set the intention to open up and expand, rather than suppress, creativity. We are all artists, poets, scientists, and lovers at heart. Many people judge themselves by the perceived quality of the outcome. Yet, mindfulness is all about the process rather than the outcome. Creativity is also more about the process than the outcome. In order to inspire you, I tried to choose images that would prove meaningful, deep, and stirring. Some are symbolic; others are archetypal; all are evocative, I hope.

As you approach the pages ahead, ask yourself: Are you willing to explore a new approach when drawing? Do you dare to take a risk? Can you let go of assumptions and expectations about who you are and what you are capable of? Are you willing to surrender completely to the process in order find out who you are and what your full potential is by engaging in the material rather than starting out with presumptions or expectations? I have purposefully collected a range of drawings that vary in content and style precisely for this reason. Some drawings include lots of open areas. Others include lots of tiny spaces. The high degree of variation plus uniqueness of each set of lines begs for your creativity in applying imagination and choosing from among a wide range of drawing techniques.

The Importance of Play!

Let yourself go. Open up your mind, body, and heart to something new. Make a mess. Splash some paint. Surrender to pure sensation. Release all expectations. Find your passion. All this and more is possible through play. Many adults assume play is reserved for little children. This is not the case at all. Within evolution, play became part of the brain circuitry of virtually every species of mammal. Through play, our brains express and exercise their open wiring. The openness of our neural circuitry allows us to learn from experience, change, discover, be flexible, improvise, be spontaneous and to innovate. There is very good reason why play is called the work of childhood! Through play comes the leading edge of growth of all kinds—behaviorally, socially, emotionally, motivationally and even intellectually. Through pretend games of imagination, children internalize the rules, roles, and relationships of the broader culture. Through play, children plant the seeds for lifelong identity, including visions about who to be and how to create a life. Although how we play shifts, the activity is equally as important for adults. Adult play sparks our vitality, humor, creativity, passion, renewal, motivation, and inspiration.

So, dear reader/drawer, I invite and even implore you to engage in this coloring book playfully. Please experiment. Take risks: some might work, some not. Just remember, there is no such thing as failure in play. There is only fun and learning without dire consequences.

HOW TO USE THIS BOOK

Please make this book your own. Approach the pages ahead in the way that most suits you. When you feel relaxed and ready to access your own creativity, you can focus on the drawings with the fewest lines and most open space. Those pages provide you with maximum freedom to add your own elements. Alternatively, if you feel stressed or preoccupied and wish only to relax, you may find it easiest to concentrate on detail already provided. Pages with lots of lines and less open space might help you to feel more held and contained.

Generally speaking, let your intuition guide you in how to move through this book. Don't be afraid to venture outside any guidelines or lines provided. Your mindful practice begins as you approach this coloring book. I encourage you to set an intention for each drawing session by consciously tuning into just what you need, both in this stage of your life as well as in this moment.

There are several options for proceeding:

- *Systematically*: by beginning at the beginning and finishing at the end;
- *Thoughtfully*: by attending to whatever quality of mindfulness you most lack or wish to cultivate in the moment;
- *Intuitively*: by honoring your current mood and internal promptings and thumbing through the pages until an image pops out (avoid thinking too hard about why);
- *Spontaneously*: by opening up to a random page and committing to its completion.
- *Playfully*: no rules or guidelines.

Whatever way you choose to proceed, notice all of your internal shifts as you move through beginning, middle and end stages of any given drawing. Try not to let your focus drift away from present-centered awareness. Instead, keep your mind riveted on what you are doing by concentrating on the content, symbolism and meaning of each drawing.

Consider how each theme fits into your life and internal processes. Highlight what you can learn about yourself as you draw. As you work on a page, feel free to augment your internal explorations with a notebook or diary. That way, you can write about each theme plus your experiences practicing mindfulness.

When you finish a drawing, make sure to sign and date it. By signing it, you take full ownership. By dating it, you can keep track of your process and progress over time. Feel free to tear out (never up!) finished pages. You can hang them up for further reflection—on your bathroom mirror, bedroom wall, or refrigerator door. Hanging your productions can serve as a reminder for continuing to self-reflect on the meaning of the drawing, either for several days or until you complete the next drawing.

If you especially like a drawing, celebrate your accomplishment by framing your piece and hanging it more permanently on your living room wall or giving it as a gift to a friend or family member. If you'd like to share a favorite drawing with me, please post it on the Facebook page I've created, called "Truly Mindful Coloring".

THERAPEUTIC APPLICATIONS

For Personal Self-Reflection and Healing

This book is designed for adults, teens, and even older children interested in drawing as a means to practice mindfulness and enhance self-awareness. Many opportunities exist in the pages ahead for self-reflection, gaining insight, becoming more internally grounded, and healing through self-expression and self-examination. Each person will naturally interact with the material differently. That's part of the fun!

Therapeutic possibilities for how to use this book are endless. Please engage your own creativity as a therapist. After having conducted open-ended psychotherapy for more than 30 years, I am deeply convinced that living creatively, in the sense of approaching each new task with novelty in mind, is at the heart of keeping life fresh and interesting for each one of us, therapists and patients alike.

Here are some circumstances when this coloring book might be particularly growth-promoting:

- When transitioning from one stage of life to another, like preparing for college, being pregnant or approaching retirement;
- When recovering from a bout of physical, mental, or neurological illness, particularly if this involves an extended stay in a hospital or treatment center;
- During a vacation or time off, especially if you yearn to gain/regain perspective on your life.

Individual Psychotherapy

If you are a psychotherapist, this coloring book makes a wonderful resource and adjunct to psychotherapy. This holds true even if you don't specialize in the expressive arts or feel especially creative yourself.

One possibility to move through the book is to choose a drawing that fits the theme of a session or a stage of your client's life or therapy. Another possibility is to let your client decide which drawing he or she most needs or wants to complete. Clients can work on drawings between sessions, and then bring them in to discuss the process later with you. Expressive arts therapists and others who work directly with creativity may prefer clients to work on drawings in their presence while simultaneously discussing themes. Talk to your patient/client in order to decide together how best to proceed.

Once a drawing is complete, you and your client/patients can extend the exploration in multiple ways. Possibilities include:

- Have clients write a poem, short essay or story, or dredge up and discuss a memory that feels personally relevant to the drawing.
- Have clients create a dance or song or find a piece of music that feels personally relevant to the drawing.
- Consider the drawing as a product of the unconscious, a kind of waking dream. Explore any and all associations that arise.
- Have clients design a follow-up drawing of their own.
- Clinical discussions can focus on the concept behind each drawing and/or the experience of mindfulness your client had (or didn't have) while working on the drawing.

Group Psychotherapy

This coloring book makes an excellent resource for group psychotherapy, whether with adults, adolescents, or even children. Possibilities include:

- Select one drawing and have all group members work on the same one simultaneously during a session. Meanwhile, talk focuses about the relevance of the theme as members draw;
- Begin with a theme for the group. Let each member individually find the drawing that best fits the theme.
- A good way to build group cohesion is for group members to start a different or even the same drawing, work on it for several minutes, and then switch drawings with other members to make collaborative creations.
- If the purpose of the group is mindfulness, then members can draw together in silence while practicing mindful drawing. Discussion would then be reserved for the end of the group only.

TIPS FOR MINDFUL DRAWING

Spiral Binder:

- Each page can be completely flattened for drawing;
- Single pages should be separated out from the rest of the book. When ready to draw, open your target page to the right and stack all other pages to the left. Place a pad or other appropriate surface under your target page. These precautions ensure that pressure marks and marker or paint colors won't bleed onto other book pages or underlying surfaces.

Possible Materials:

- Colored pencils: great for shading and blending;
- Artist pens: vibrant colors; tiny tips available; pen sets often come with blenders;
- Gel markers: greatest pizzazz, especially with metallic and glitter colors;
- Gouache or oil pastels: good for coloring large areas, easily blending colors, as well as for coloring over black lines;
- Experiment by mixing multiple media within a single drawing.

Anyone New to Art:

- Colored pencils are best for starting and experimenting;
- Hold colored pencils, markers, or gel pens just like a regular pencil.
- Practice first by taking a blank piece of paper and making a series of straight lines, circles, squares, and other shapes, just to give yourself a feel for freehand drawing.
- Remember: practice may not make perfect, but it will make all the difference! Your mind/body/brain unity will naturally shift and progress the more time you put in playing with the materials.
- People new to coloring books often choose realistic palettes, while those with more experience become bolder in color choice. Follow your heart.
- Above all, drop your expectations. Have fun and listen to your instincts. You will quickly and easily feel progress in how you see and approach the pages.

TIPS FOR COLORED PENCILS

- Make sure colored pencils are always sharpened. Begin each session with the ritual of sharpening the palette of colors you intend to work with. If possible, use an Exacto knife rather than a pencil sharpener. Sharpen by shaving off flakes round and round the pencil until it comes to a perfect point.
- Work in layers
  - Press lightly and evenly, using broad strokes for open areas;
  - Build thin layers of color, one by one, using soft pressure to fill in white spaces;
  - Color all areas within the entire page before moving onto the next layer;
  - This technique keeps the whole in mind when deciding about color choice or how much pressure to apply to different areas.

- Pressure
  - Achieve a soft effect by never applying hard pressure. Instead, use a Kleenex or blending stick to remove remaining white spaces;

  - Achieve a bright effect by applying hard pressure to eliminate all white spaces in the final layer;

- To achieve a faded-out effect, apply fewer and fewer layers towards the edges.

- Shading
  - Achieve a 3-D effect by shading with graphite or colored pencils.

- Use either a regular, graphite pencil or a darker color toward the edges of figures combined with a lighter color towards the inside.
- For the top layer, you can use the lightest color throughout to unify the object or area.
- Here are four different techniques of shading:

Blending

Hatching

Cross-Hatching

Stippling

- Blending colors
  - In some areas (or whole drawings), use the same color for multiple layers in order to achieve bright, pure or primary color;

  - In other areas (or drawings), mix different colors in different layers in order to achieve a more complex look;

  - In order to get a translucent effect, e.g., for skin tones, use a dark color in the bottom layers and finish by pressing hard with a very light color.

GENERAL PREPARATION:

- Begin by *emptying your mind* of all thoughts and residues from the day. Use the ritual of sharpening your pencils or gathering your materials to draw a crisp line between all that has come before and what you are about to do.
- It helps to choose a special place or sacred spot in which to draw. To further aid preparation, each chapter offers a brief guided meditation.

- Before beginning a new drawing, *first take a long, careful look at the page*. Let it speak to you. What does it have to say? What emotions does it evoke? What might be missing in the lines? How can you play with the image?

- Alongside color choices, look in order to see what lines, patterns, or themes, if any, you might like to add. This is especially important for pages with wide open spaces. Once your imagination speaks to you, use a pencil or black marker to add your own lines and patterns prior to filling in any colors.

- Choose your color palette ahead of time by looking at the page and then pulling out the pencils or markers you wish to use. Be brave in choosing your palette! Remember that your palette doesn't need to resemble reality.

- As you work, *feel free to venture outside the lines*. When tackling areas such as hair or clouds, you can add a special touch by having the color slightly extend beyond the lines. Likewise, let yourself be adventuresome inside the lines.

- *Put aside your inner critic*. Remember there is no right or wrong to the process. The idea is to cultivate qualities of mind, rather than to produce amazing works of art. Even if you wind up unhappy with how a drawing turns out, you can utilize your experience productively. Consider it an opportunity to work with inner demons or a learning experience to capitalize on in the future. This attitude helps you maintain a *growth mindset* throughout.

- As you draw, practice *dual awareness* by shuttling your attention back and forth between internal experiences—body experiences, feelings, thoughts—and external experiences—perceptions, sensations and observations. Especially when practicing mindfulness with your eyes open, many teachers of these practices consider dual awareness at the heart of true mindfulness.

- If your main intention is to relax, a good way to cultivate calm and internal grounding is *to become aware of your breath*. The first step is simply to notice how you are breathing. Are you taking nice long inhalations and exhalations or are you breathing quickly and shallowly—a classic sign of anxiety, stress, and hyperarousal? The second step is to lengthen inhalations and especially exhalations for greatest relaxation. As you draw, you can even coordinate your breath with arm and hand movements.

- Whether or not you choose to coordinate with the breath, let yourself be conscious of finding a rhythmic flow with your pencil strokes. This will help with fluidity, grace, and flow, while drawing unnecessary thoughts right out of your head.

- If you wish to add music, feel free, but do so thoughtfully. Choose music that fits the theme or quality of awareness you are attempting to cultivate. Find the quality of movement throughout your arm and hand that adds to the mood and content of your reflections, rather than takes you away from them. You can even try coordinating your hand strokes to the beat of the music.

Please visit the book's website (www.TrulyMindfulColoring.com) for products and tips related to this coloring book. Visit the book's Facebook page (www.facebook.com/TrulyMindfulColoring) to create a community filled with inspiration and shared drawings, comments and personal experiences. You can contact me directly at TrulyMindfulColoring@hotmail.com.

It's time to have fun drawing!

CHAPTER ONE

Creating Inner Refuge
through Stilling the Mind

The mindfulness movement emerged largely from ancient meditation practices. A still mind won't cure all problems, leave you free from concerns, or alleviate difficult emotions, but it can maximize your chances for inner peace and contentment. A still mind allows you to seek the center of your being, deep below the hustle and bustle of everyday life. By separating the essence of who you are from your circumstances and the ongoing flux of perceptions and emotions, you can take refuge at the still center of pure consciousness.

When approaching the drawings in this chapter, please contemplate and practice your capacity for inner stillness. After collecting your materials, sharpening your pencils, and finding the right spot in which to draw, here is a guided meditation (adapted from Marks-Tarlow, 2014) to help still your mind:

Imagine yourself as a mountain standing tall in the sky, yet firmly grounded. Feel your solidity and connection to the Earth. Sense the quality of your terrain—whether it is rugged or smooth; whether it is pure or covered with brush and trees. Experience the mountain as your still place. Now picture the continual fluctuation of your internal experience as the weather pattern that surrounds the mountain. Some thoughts and feelings will hang like wispy clouds on the very peaks of the mountain. Some will envelop the entire mountain. Some conditions will be stormy. There may be thunder, lightning, and strong winds. Some conditions will be like fog or dark, ominous clouds. On cloudless days, the clarity of perspective can be breath-taking, with a 360 degree view of the surrounding area. At certain times of the year, the weather conditions will hang around for quite a while, like a storm that rages on for days. At other times of the year, the change in weather patterns may be rapid or sudden. Whatever your experience of these patterns, the weather that surrounds the mountain will always remain in flux, while the mountain itself will always remain steady, still, and solid beneath it all. As you experience the contrast between the mountain and its weather patterns, feel free to inhale the word 'mountain,' and exhale the word 'still', 'stable', or 'solid.' Whether or not you choose to attach words, use the breath to focus on the present climate. This will expand and your capacity to weather the storm like a mountain that stands strong and connected to the earth.

If you find yourself swept up in a thought or emotion, notice it and simply let it pass. The key is to pay attention to the ever-changing process of thinking, feeling, and sensing as if witnessing clouds floating through, rather than allowing yourself to get caught up and carried away with the contents of your thoughts. As you begin to see the contents of your consciousness as ethereal and mere wisps of experience, any particular thought, sensation or emotion will start to lose its power to define the whole of you.

To sit still with the intention of stilling the mind is one of the simplest acts we can undertake. Yet, this can be one of the hardest things to do. Although drawing requires movement, a still mind can help you to achieve states of flow. The more you get into flow states throughout your life, the easier it will be to still the body and mind at the same time.

As you draw these seated Buddhas, contemplate the stillness that resides within you. If you notice any blocks to stillness, see if you can let them pass through like wispy clouds passing a mountain in the sky.

Wheel of Awareness

This Colossal Wheel was fashioned after a 13th century temple relief located in Orissa, India. Twelve pairs of intricately decorated wheels transport the Chariot of the Sun as drawn by seven spirited horses. The hub of the Colossal Wheel represents the still point at the center of the self. At the rim surrounding this still hub, the rest of life's drama circles round and round.

As you fill in this image, let yourself feel the difference between operating close to the still point in the center of your being versus getting pulled round and round by drama and the dizzying pace of operating at the rim. As you drift away from your internal center, try to isolate what is happening, not just in your mind, but also in your body. What pulls you away—Fear? Overwhelm? Boredom? Restlessness? Or something else? Where do you hold these things in your body?

Most importantly, how can you bring yourself back to the center of your being?

An ancient Zen teaching tale speaks of a master and student sharing a cup of tea. While the student talks incessantly, the master pours the tea over the rim, allowing it to spill on the table and eventually onto the floor. "What are you doing?" cried the student. "Only by emptying the cup of your mind will you have room for anything new!" exclaimed the Master. Likewise, by striving to empty our minds of all preconceived notions, assumptions, and expectations, we can carry a beginner's mind to everything we do, no matter what our level of expertise, no matter how many times we have done it before.

As you approach this image of Baby Bud, empty your mind of all preconceptions, expectations, and previous experience with drawing and/or art. Instead, let yourself dwell on the sweet innocence of infancy and early childhood. Allow the image of the baby you were and the babies you've known help you tap into beginner's mind.

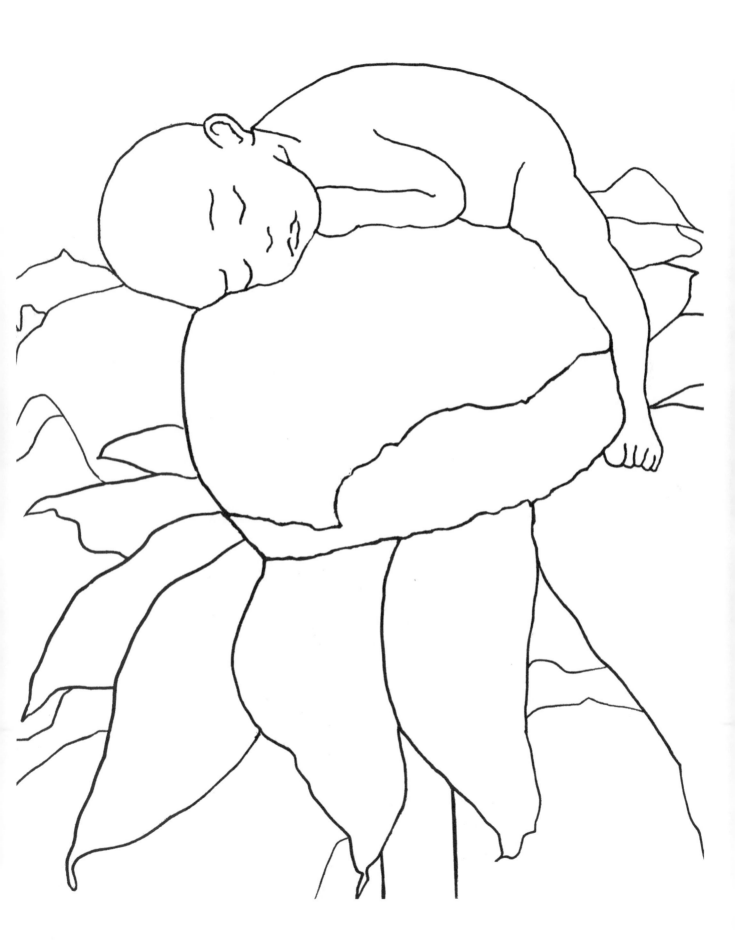

If something internal blocks your capacity for beginner's mind or to achieve joy in life, it is probably your inner critic. This is the inner voice that judges and scolds us for not being good, pretty, productive, or successful enough. This voice often mirrors the voice of a critical parent. The tone and content can range from gentle criticism to outright self-hatred. While an abusive tone is never helpful, such voices don't need to be permanently silenced. When compassionately expressed, they warn us if we are headed off track or have made a mistake. Yet, it is important to separate out the ground of our being from the reach of these voices.

Especially with respect to art, our inner critic often hovers nearby. As you fill in this image, see if you can silence self-criticism. First, listen to what your inner voice is trying to tell you, and then try answering aloud. You might emphasize that your intention is to achieve inner peace rather than a skilled or beautiful outcome.

Staying Present

What is your relationship with time? Are you focused more in the past by reviewing memories, regrets, or barraged by "woulda, shoulda, couldas"? Alternatively, are you riveted more in the future by pressures, plans, and worries about what's to come? Either position, as a fixed stance, will prevent you from remaining present. The idea isn't to forget the past or future, but to stay completely engaged in whatever you are doing, while holding everything else lightly, in the background of awareness.

As you approach this fractal watch, try to enhance your present-centered awareness. Contemplate your relationship to time. Are you more likely to get stuck in the past, as in depression, or the future, as in anxiety? One way to bring yourself back from either stance is to focus on bodily sensations and perceptions. This can instantly ground you in present-centered experience.

Self-Control

In many ways, mindfulness practices promote self-control. Yet, the notion that we are totally in control of anything in our lives, including our minds, bodies, or relationships, is purely an illusion. Our conscious will and decision-making never fully controls our emotions or bodily states. To tame the mind and quiet an aroused nervous system takes patience and discipline, much like taming a wild animal. Even if the animal eventually becomes docile, we must always respect its wild nature.

Through mindfulness practices, we strive to cultivate discipline and patience and cooperate with our minds, brains, and bodies, partly by honoring and surrendering to that which lies beyond our control. As you approach this drawing, contemplate the quality of your will and discipline, plus where you struggle to assert self-control. When addressing these issues, it is usually more effective to strive and shift in tiny steps rather than huge leaps, lest we get too tangled in strings of our own self-deception.

When we tune into the workings of our minds, we loop processes of awareness from what is outside of us to what is going on internally. We watch ourselves, and then we watch ourselves watching ourselves, and so on. The more we sit still and reflect inwards, the greater the potential for depth. The infinite depth that is possible when we truly face our selves resembles the infinite recursion of our own image as we stand between two mirrors that face one another.

As you complete this drawing, contemplate your quality of self-reflection. Are you comfortable being alone? Do you enjoy your own company? What blocks you from staying aware of and self-reflective about your own emotional and relational experiences? How can you address those blocks?

Polarities

Deep within every psyche exists a double aspect—a set of opposites that contradict yet intertwine and interpenetrate, like the two sides of the yin/yang. Each side "opposes" the other, yet each contains seeds of the other within the center of its being. Inner refuge depends upon accepting and working with this balance of opposites, even for detestable qualities like good/evil.

Please complete this drawing by engaging your wildest imagination to dress, decorate, doodle and otherwise enjoy the play of contrasts. Meanwhile, conjure up all of the opposite qualities inside of yourself. What blocks you from valuing both sides of every polarity? It is all too easy to accept only one side and reject the other.

Remember, especially for unwanted aspects, that accepting and working with an undesirable aspect of yourself is very different from endorsing or condoning it. Only by accepting all of ourselves can we hope to change any part of ourselves.

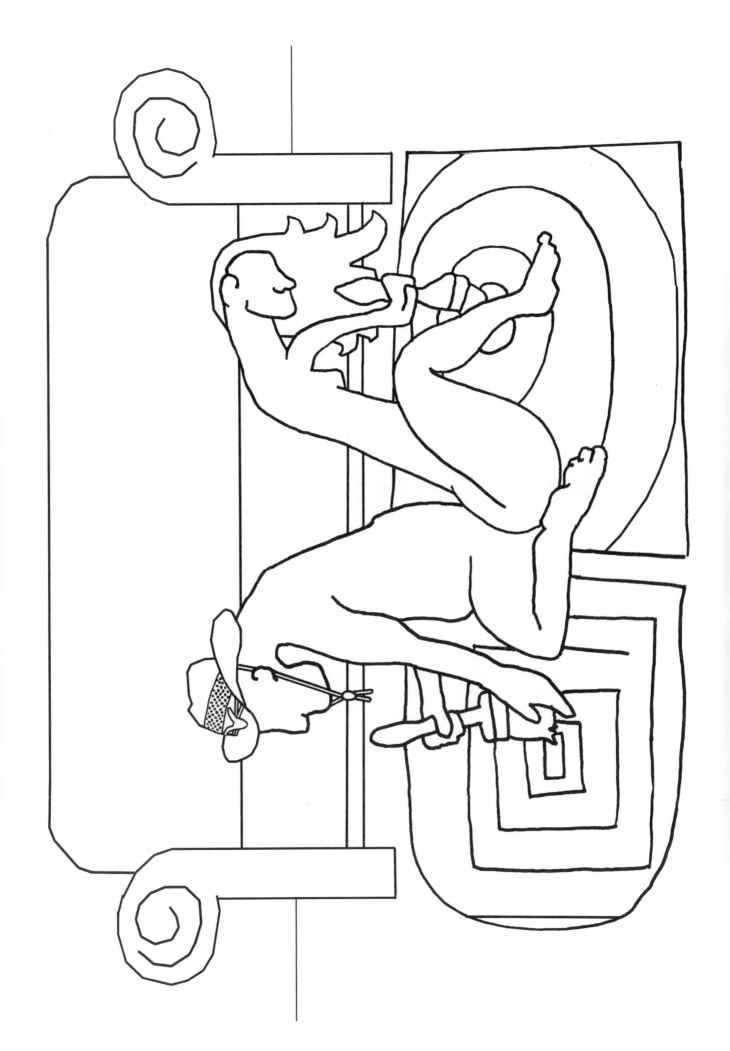

I/Eye of Self-Awareness

Simply to utter the word "I" is a self-referential act. Our inner eye, or "witness consciousness," is that part of ourselves able to stand back and watch what is going on. Yet trying to capture all of our truths this way is much like turning the eye turning in its own socket. There will always be a blind spot. The more you refuse to accept the polarities that reside within you, the larger your blind spot may be.

As you complete Maurice Escher's art gallery on the left and David Hockney's self-referential canvas on the right, contemplate your own blind spots—aspects of your unconscious that you are destined never to see. A word of caution here: if you believe you know yourself so well that you have no blind spots, then you have found your blind spot right there!

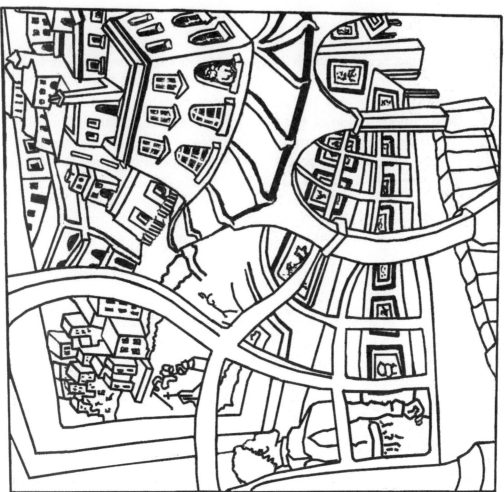

Two Brains/
Two Selves

Each human brain is divided in into two sides, or hemispheres. We associate the left half of the brain (right side of the body) with our conscious sense of self and verbal stories. Meanwhile, the right half of the brain (left side of the body) provides the minute-to-minute, nonverbal, sensory, emotional, and relational ground of our being, as well as the origins of nonconscious experience, including our "blind spots," where we are blocked from insight.

Mindfulness meditation often strives to silence the verbal left in order to bring forward the more embodied right. This drawing reveals what can happen if the two halves of the brain do not cooperate well with one another.

As you color in this drawing, please take note of the two perspectives afforded by your right and left hemispheres, plus your degree of integration. To mix things up, experiment by using your non-dominant hand to draw.

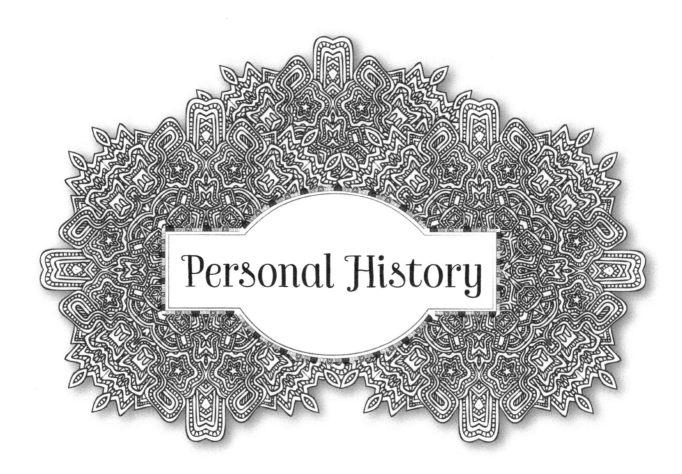

Personal History

Each one of us carries a unique personal history. Some of us are born into privilege, others into hardship. No matter what our circumstances, everyone suffers losses, if not trauma. An important aspect of cultivating inner equanimity is to understand the role personal history plays in your life. Most people do the best they can with the resources they have. Lots of problems persist if we hold onto outdated coping. The best way to change ourselves is to come to grips with how we got to be exactly where and who we are now.

As you complete this drawing of a woman perched between a rock and a hard place, please review the various stages of your life to date. Consider whether you have made peace with the events of the past.

If not, what interferes? If you feel like a victim of your own history, how can you move past this stance? Is it possible to do so without needing anything external from anyone or anything? What stops you from acting on what you know?

In many of the world's myths, land symbolizes the conscious mind, while water symbolizes the unconscious. Turbulent water is difficult to see through, while still water lends clarity and mirrors what lies in the depths as well as that which is reflected on the surface. This kind of dual consciousness—of what is on the surface and what lies underneath in the depths—is the essence of a mindful approach to life.

As you color this page, reflect on your own qualities of mind like water. Does your psyche feel turbulent or clear? If turbulent, what do you need to help still the well? Feel free to add lines and images of your own before coloring.

CHAPTER TWO

Focusing Your Mind into Laser Beam Attention

Over and over, times arise in life when it is important to clear everything out of the periphery of attention. By narrowing your focus to a single point, your attention can function like a laser beam whose incisive power stems from its singular direction. A focused mind lends purpose and momentum to take action and complete tasks. The opposite of flighty attention or a fidgety body, a focused mind remains strong and steady like steel—ready to endure challenge and face adversity without distraction. Many types of meditation restrict attention to a narrow band, like gazing at a lit candle, conjuring up a single image, repeating a mantra, or singing a chant.

When approaching the drawings in this module, please contemplate and practice your capacity for laser beam attention. After collecting your materials, sharpening your pencils, and finding the right spot in which to draw, here is a guided meditation (adapted from Marks-Tarlow, 2014) that centers on bodily awareness and the breath to help focus your mind:

Close your eyes and begin with a scan of your body. How are you feeling inside? What sensations present themselves to you? Sense the clothes on your body and support of your chair. Now follow your breath. Notice your abdomen and chest expanding during each inhalation. Feel your belly and chest contracting during each exhalation. Sense the continuous waves of breath like the waves of the sea. As you lengthen and deepen each breath, become so internally engaged that you surrender to the process completely. Immerse yourself in your physical sensations and your breath until no words move through your mind. If thoughts do enter, carefully set them aside for later. Do several rounds of deep breathing, feeling your inhalations moving from your nostrils all the way into your belly and then making sure to exhale all of the air out your belly and lungs completely. After completing several rounds and getting a good rhythm going, combine your breathing with a body scan. Start with your feet, one at a time. Inhale relaxation into each foot, and exhale tension out, imagine it dropping into the ground. Work your way up through your legs and torso slowly, one area at a time, breathing in relaxation, breathing out tension. Include the inner organs of your heart, lungs, and digestive system, as well as your arms, neck, and face. Move through your body slowly until you reach the very top of your head, visualizing each area clearly along the way. Once you have finished your body scan, feel the unity of your body. Feel the breath moving throughout your whole body at once. Blend so fully with your breath that nothing separates you from it. Allow yourself to move from you doing the breathing to your breath breathing you into life. Allow yourself to BECOME THE BREATH. Take as many more rounds as you wish this way, staying as inwardly focused and engaged as you possibly can. Then, whenever you are ready, open your eyes and return to the room.

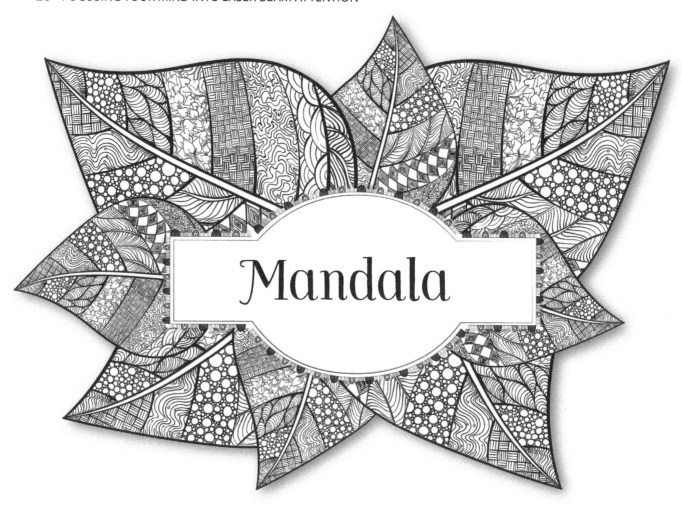

Mandala

The mandala appears in many cultures as an ancient symbol for the totality of the cosmos. In India, mandalas are frequently created ritualistically in the sand and then allowed to be blown away by the winds of time. Psychologically, mandalas reflect outer worlds at the very same time as they reflect inner worlds—the deepest layer where inner and outer connect and are continuous with one another. Freud's early disciple, Carl Jung, viewed the squared circle of the mandala as a symbol for how the little self of the conscious ego meets the big self of spirit and universal consciousness.

As you work on this drawing, focus your mind on your spiritual dimension. Whether or not you practice a formal religion or believe in God, we all have a spiritual dimension. How do you understand and meet the totality of the universe? If inspired, when you finish this drawing, please create and color your own version next.

This page derives from a sculptural relief found at Angkor Wat, one of the world's seven wonders located in Cambodia. Though filled with detail, there are also lots of ambiguous areas lacking clear shape. Where do the lines represent abstract patterns versus concrete images? In daily life, many people get easily frustrated with ambiguity. They want everything to be crystal clear. Unfortunately, that's not how the universe operates. Especially with respect to big concerns in life, so often we must keep our focus on the details while patiently awaiting the resolution of ambiguity.

This drawing moves the mind towards laser beam focus on detail, with an open invitation to interpret and color each area in the manner most meaningful to you.

As you color in this page, focus your mind on all that is ambiguous and not fully formed in your own life. How do you feel about the ambiguity? Does it trigger continual frustration or a sense of potential? What makes the difference between these two stances? See what arises as you contemplate these matters.

Along with ambiguity, the universe is filled with uncertainty. We might wish for full certainty, yet if our lives were fully scripted and predictable, we could easily become bored and would hardly need to show up. Precisely because our lives are filled with chaos, we must stay awake to face life's dramas. No amount of wealth or privilege protects us from this existential reality.

In many of the world's cultures, the dragon symbolizes chaos. The poet Rainer Maria Rilke suggested, "Perhaps all the dragons in our lives are princesses, who are only waiting to see us act, just once with beauty and courage. Perhaps everything that frightens us is, in its deepest essence, something helpless that wants our attention."

As you work on this drawing, contemplate all the chaos that exists in your life. How can you meet your fears head on, instead of running away, becoming paralyzed, or simply wishing the nastiness would all go away? Keep in mind that courage isn't the absence of fear, but the conviction to move forward anyway.

Because of the suffering inherent in living, some spiritual texts portray life itself as a battlefield, as in this this image, "Crossing the Red Sea," drawn from a medieval panel. To steel up our minds, fight the dragon of chaos, and deal with whatever may come, it helps to adopt what I call a "warrior's stance." We can ready ourselves for anything in life by learning from experience and then trusting in our present-centered capacities to handle whatever comes our way. To adopt a warrior's stance is partly not to have to know what is coming next. This helps to reduce the continual churn of worry that surrounds all of those "what-if?" scenarios we can spin out with. Be mindful about choosing the warrior's stance as a conscious way to face transitional times and difficult moments, rather than as an ongoing state of braced or defended being.

As you color in the detail of this drawing, reflect upon the stages of your own life. Meditate on whether you have adopted a warrior's stance. If something blocks your way, what is it? How can you address any obstacles?

Wisdom of Insecurity

In Western mythology, humankind typically must fight and defeat the dragon of chaos in order to establish civilization and preserve its order. In Eastern and more traditional and indigenous cultures, no clear divide exists between chaos and order or within other polarities, such as good/bad or truth/falsity. This is much like the yin/yang symbol, where the seeds of each opposite are planted in the center of the other.

Rather than killing the dragon of chaos, humankind works hand in hand with it instead. Look closely to see that the Chinese dragon pictured here, which lives in the clouds and makes thunder with its feet, also guards pearls of wisdom.

As you color in this page, contemplate how to work more closely with the dragons of chaos in your life. What pearls of wisdom might emerge from greater cooperation?

The Oroboros, or snake that swallows its tail, is an ancient symbol of self-fertilization and creative regeneration. By bending so fully around, the Oroboros begins anew every time it reaches its end.

Symbolically, the Oroboros helps us to tame chaos by taking in feedback and changing according to what is learned, on the basis of new information. This is how our brains, bodies, and minds remain flexible to grow and change with each new cycle of experience.

As you fill in this page, focus on important matters of growth, change, and processes of self-renewal in your own life.

Double Oroboros

The double Oroboros symbolizes mutual feedback and cycles of interdependence between people, animals, and other aspects of nature. We don't live in a vacuum, yet all too easily have the experience of being independent and completely separate from others. To the contrary, most of us remain dependent upon others for what we eat and wear, where we live, what music we listen to, and for every other aspect of culture we enjoy. Alongside this material level of interdependence, it is healthy to lean on others emotionally, not just in childhood, but throughout life.

As you work on this drawing, consider mutual feedback loops and cycles of interdependence you have with others, especially your most intimate relationships. Does the level of mutual dependence feel healthy and reciprocal? If not, what do you need to adjust or change? Are you ready to begin now?

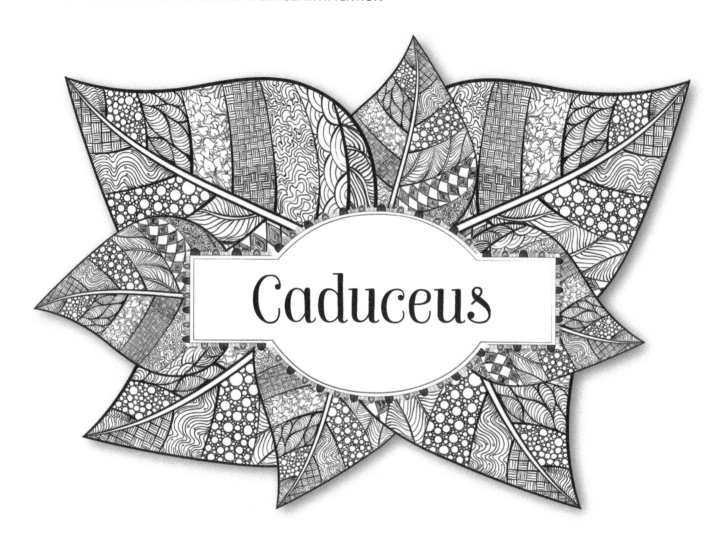

Caduceus

The symbol of the snake is filled with opposites, because its venom is both poison and cure at the very same time. We have all heard the expression, "That which doesn't kill us will make us stronger."

In this drawing, the dual quality of hurting/healing is reflected by two intertwined snakes that form the Caduceus, or healer's staff, ancient symbol of Western medicine.

As you complete this drawing, please meditate on how the problems and stresses of your life can serve to strengthen and even heal you.

The Shadow

When we stand in sunlight, a shadow follows us everywhere. Likewise, once we open ourselves up to the light of self-reflection, we must learn how to face negative aspects of ourselves that are ugly, unwanted, and even evil. Light and darkness always operate hand in hand.

A mindful approach helps us to gaze upon and work with the dark side of ourselves, by bringing understanding and compassion to self-examination. The more we accept and allow in the unwanted side of ourselves, the more whole we become and suffused with light. As a beautiful line by Leonard Cohen states, "There is a crack in everything; that's how the light gets in."

As you color in this drawing, please add elements that relate to your shadow side. Contemplate how you can face and accept the dark side of yourself more fully.

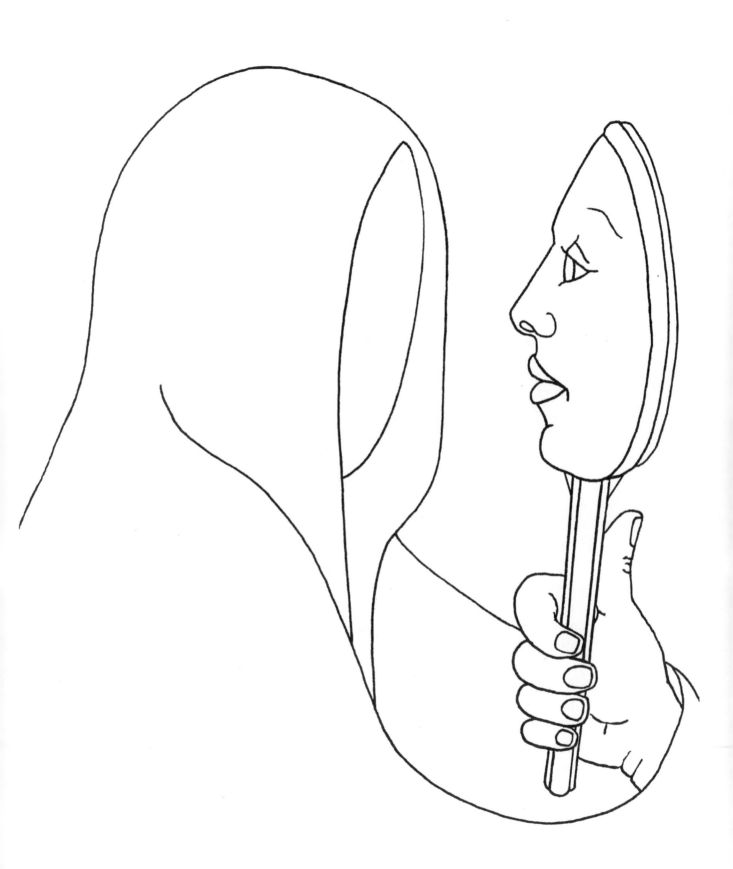

Corridors

As we walk the path of our lives, we cross many thresholds, while making transition after transition. All our feelings, relationships, circumstances in life, and even the very cells that occupy our bodies and brains are transient to one degree or other. The more we can focus in on details of these pivot points, the more flexible and adaptable our minds become.

As you complete this drawing, contemplate the change points in your life. Do you detect any repeating patterns? Do you tend to bound blindly over new thresholds? Do you step cautiously? Do you hold back out of fear, avoiding even necessary changes? Are you comfortable and satisfied with how you approach transitions and pivot points in your life? If not, how would you like to tweak or refine your style?

Labyrinth

The labyrinth is an ancient symbol of the spiritual journey into the center of the self and back out again, into the world. The path twists and turns and is filled with lots of dead ends.

As you complete this drawing, contemplate the meaning of this symbol for yourself in the labyrinth of your own life.

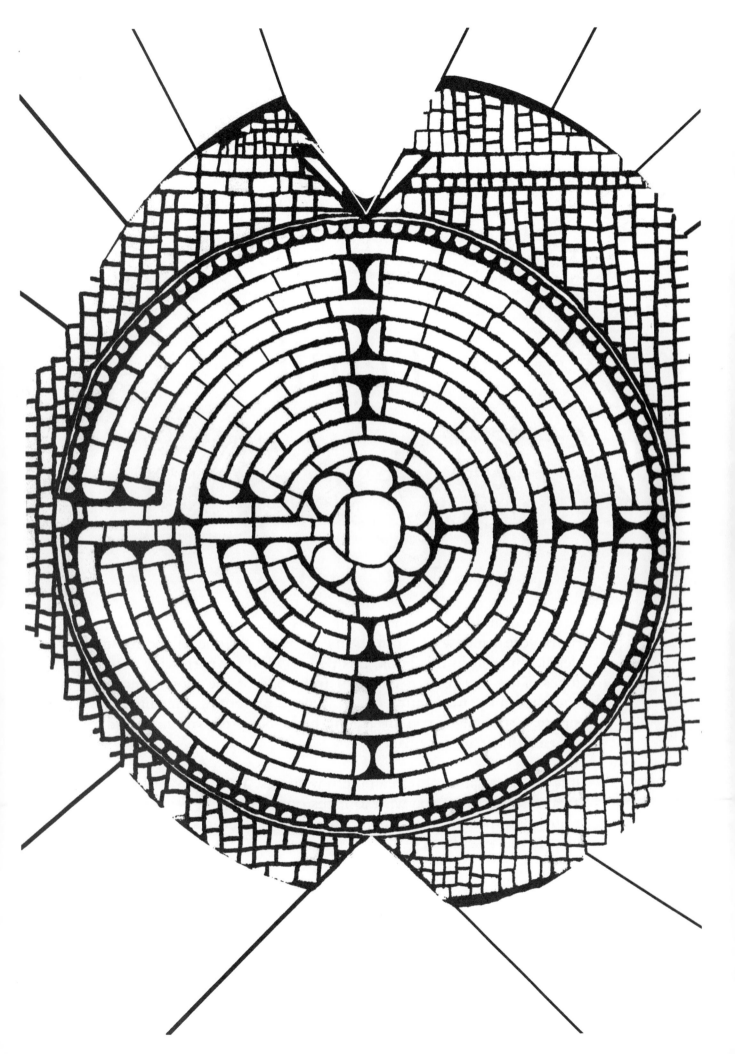

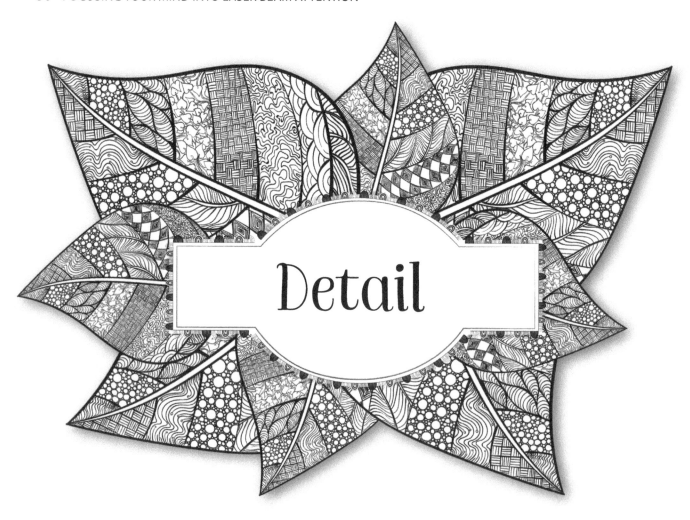

A focused mind zooms into detail. This image is drawn from the north rose window of Notre Dame in Paris. As one of the most detailed images in this book, this page is ideal for narrowing your focus. That this pattern is drawn from one of the most famous churches in the world attests to its value in promoting a meditative stance. Especially if you are feeling highly stressed, you may find yourself drawn to this image.

It is not necessary to fill in all the tiny spaces. You can color broad areas instead. But if you wish to focus on the detail, it helps to use really sharp pencils or tiny tip gel pens, perhaps even a magnifying glass in the other hand.

As you work with this image, contemplate the ways in which your daily spirituality provides you opportunities to focus your attention and appreciate the small details of life.

CHAPTER THREE

Cultivating an Open, Receptive Mind

An open mind is soft and receptive—quite the opposite from a focused mind that is directed and pointed. An open mind requires broadband attention that fans out in all directions at once to spread its soft focus far and wide. In order to cultivate an open mind, you must set aside all expectations, desires, fears, and intentions. This allows you to open up to novelty and to whatever spontaneously arises within and around you. To refrain from moving your attention in any deliberate direction is to heighten your receptivity to what already is present in each moment. There are many situations in which an open mind is helpful, such as meeting a new person, conducting psychotherapy, or entering a place where you wish to take in novelty, like a museum or new country. An open mind is also important whenever you wish to scan the whole of things, such as walking through nature.

The drawings in this chapter help you practice your capacity for receptivity. After collecting your materials, sharpening your pencils, and finding the right spot in which to draw, here is a guided meditation (adapted from Marks-Tarlow, 2014) to help open your mind:

Start by tilting your head slightly upwards to find a spot, feature or other point on the ceiling to gaze at. Zoom in to notice details of what you see—textures, colors, other qualities. Now do the opposite by softening your eyes in order to take in the space between that point on the ceiling and your own eyes. Next, let your eyes drift closed. Once you close your outer eyes, open the inner eyes of your imagination in order to find the space between your two eyes. Take a couple of breaths to expand your focus there. Then move your attention into the space inside your nose and breath into the space between your nostrils. As you continue moving your focus this way, slow the pace of your breathing and use each breath to spread luxuriously into these spaces. Next find the space between your ears. See if you can pulsate that space with any sounds you hear or with the rhythm of your heart or any inner sounds. Next, move your attention to the space inside your throat. With each inhalation and exhalation feel this space expanding. Then find the space between your shoulders. Then within your rib cage. Feel your heart expanding. Now find the space inside your stomach. Then between your hips. Now move your attention to your hands. First find the space between the thumb and first finger on each hand, then between each of the other fingers, then between tips of your fingers and your wrists. Now find the space between your wrists and elbows. Now between your pelvis and knees. Now between your knees and feet. Now find the space between each toe. Once you have found and expanded all of these internal spaces, expand your scope of awareness to include all of the spaces inside your body at once. Now open up again to include the spaces that exist outside of your body. Imagine the boundary between the two kinds of spaces dissolving into one continuous space. Let your open awareness rest in that extended space for as long as you would like. Notice whatever sensations and emotions come up as you do. When you feel ready to return to the room, first bring your focus back to one point in the space between your eyes. Then slowly inhabit your eyes, until you feel ready to open them.

Tree of Life

The Tree of Life as a symbol appears in Mayan mythology at the locus of creation, in Egyptian mythology as the place where life and death coincide, and in the Garden of Eden alongside the Tree of Knowledge. Across different cultures and eras, the Tree of Life represents the mystical, complex, interconnected web of life.

As you complete this drawing, please open your mind wide to consider what the Tree of Life means to you.

Nature is an open system with open borders. Each aspect of nature is intimately related to every other aspect. We humans are not separate from our mammal relatives, but instead are intimately connected. In fact, we are way more similar than different from our surroundings.

Consider that we share 50% of our genes with a banana. We share over 99% of our DNA with our simian cousins.

As you complete this drawing of a spider monkey and baby, contemplate your open-mindedness by feeling and considering your similarities and connections to mammals and other animals.

From the perspective of the body, an open stance in life is a stance of embrace. The more we embrace all of what we sense, feel, and experience around us—whether positive or negative—the more inner riches we can gather.

We don't have to like or approve of something in order to embrace it, we just have to be open to dealing with it. The more we embrace our struggles, the more our enemies, losses, and other sources of pain can serve as our teachers.

As you approach this image, consider your own openness to embracing all of life, including your challenges and problems. Notice that which you resist embracing. What stops you? Where do you hold the resistance in your body? Is there some way to soften those places?

Eye of Horus

The Eye of Horus is a symbol of protection from ancient Egypt. It consists of six parts that correspond to the six senses of touch, taste, hearing, thought, sight, and smell.

Sensory data is considered "food" for the Eye of Horus, whose all-seeing quality serves as a perfect symbol for an open mind.

As you color in this drawing, consider each of your six senses as the embodied aspect of mindfulness. Try to tap into each sense, one at a time, in order to open it as wide as possible. Let yourself feel deeply in your body what it means to open wide each of the senses.

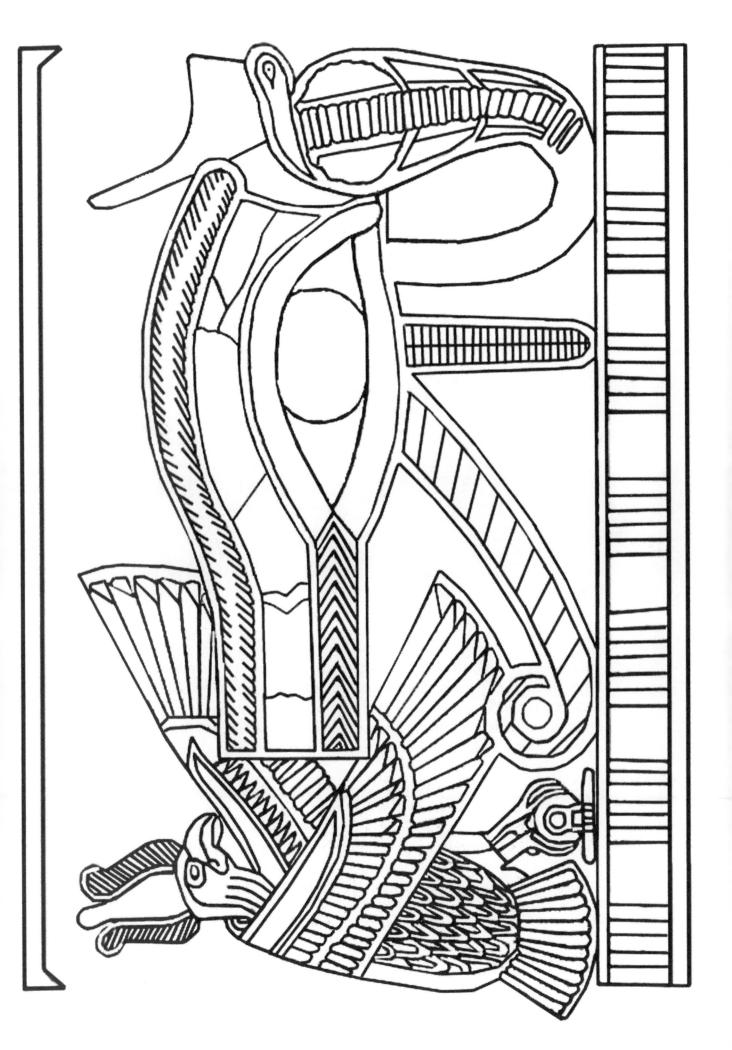

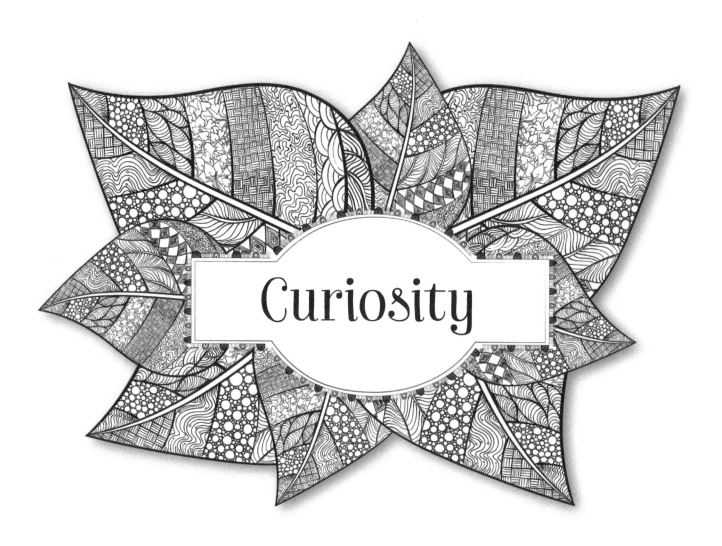

Curiosity is the hallmark of an open mind. When we are curious and take interest in people, culture and other aspects of the world around us, we naturally take in new sights, sounds, and information. Little children love to peer under rocks to discover new things. They also ask "Why?" over and over. Curiosity is built into young minds and bodies.

The more we hold onto and cultivate this quality as we grow and age, the more expansive our lives will remain.

As you color in this drawing, contemplate the quality of your curiosity. Have you retained passionate interest in life? If so, where and how does it get most ignited? If not, when did it get lost? What can you do to regain this aspect of your vitality?

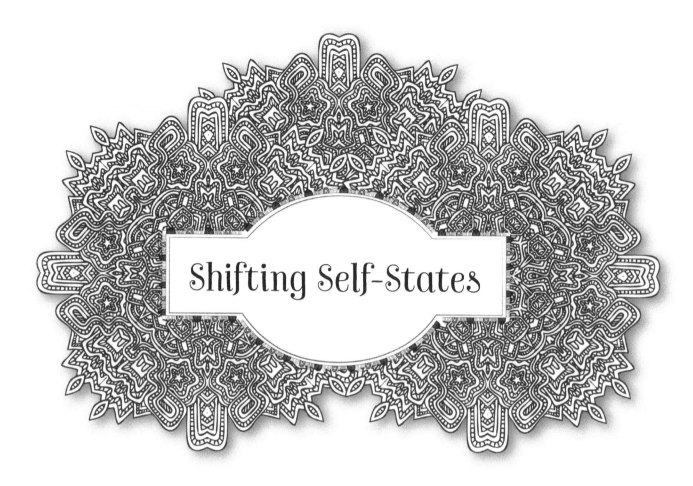

Shifting Self-States

As we move through the hours, weeks, and years of our lives, our moods, feelings, thoughts, and sensibilities remain in continual flux. This may feel uncomfortable at times, but helps us stay attuned to a dynamic, ever-changing world, both inside and outside us. Some people chase happiness as a steady state, as if they can put an end to angst or sadness for all time.

Alas, this is not how the mind works! There is a time and place for each emotion, both negative and positive. We all require the full range of states to maintain a healthy, responsive mind and body.

As you complete this drawing, consider your openness to all that you feel. Do you let in grief and anger, alongside joy and excitement? Do your emotions shift fluidly and adaptively? Do you tend to get stuck on any particular emotion or end of the negative-positive spectrum? If so, how can you promote a more balanced repertoire?

Why did Humpty Dumpty fall off the wall? Why couldn't all the King's horses and all the King's men put him back together again? Maybe this tragedy happened because Humpty Dumpty was a brittle, fragile egg who lacked resilience. When we are open to all that life offers, we tumble and fall, only to brush ourselves off again, learn from the experience, and get back on our feet over and over. We may dream of getting things right and perfect the first time, but this is unrealistic. Instead, resilience is a central quality of mind, body, and determination that helps us endure discouragement and achieve success in the long run.

As you color this drawing, consider adding elements to increase Humpty's resilience and possibly even prevent his tragic end. Where and how you have been resilient in your life? If the word "failure" is part of your self-talk, how can you switch over to a growth mindset?

From a growth perspective, we must occasionally learn what doesn't work in order to try something else in the future.

When we are resilient, engage our passions, and remain open to all that life offers, we maximize our chances of flow. Flow means that we are so fully immersed in what we are doing as to easily lose track of time and everything else outside our immediate focus. Because flow is an open stance, we don't fight or resist any part of our experience, but instead get effortlessly carried along by its currents.

As you work on this drawing of the ancient Indian figure, Kokopelli, consider the rhythms of your life. Do you move with the natural flows around you? What activities leave you most open to achieving this state of mind/body/brain unity? Do you sometimes find yourself moving against the flow, as if fighting what you are doing or trying to swim upstream?

If so, how can you turn around and ease your energy output to better harmonize with the natural currents both inside and around you?

Plato said, "Music gives a soul to the universe, wings to the mind, flight to the imagination, and life to everything." Some people consider music to be the oldest language. Evidence for musical instruments exists from prehistoric times, well before the spoken word. All cultures have music. As babies, we are moved by music, even in the womb. As we grow, most of us mark significant memories by the music we listen to.

By opening ourselves to music, we open up to rhythm, flow and the emotional undercurrents of relationships. Music is a universal language that helps to entrain us to our internal, biological rhythms as well as to coordinate our personal rhythms with those of the people around us.

As you color this image, put on meaningful music that suits your current mood. As you listen, coordinate the rhythm of your hand to that of the beat. Muse over various stages of your life as reflected by changes in your musical tastes? How do these changes reflect who you were before and who you have become now?

We all have rituals in our lives. Some are prescribed by society, parents, or religion. Others we develop on our own. Rituals allow us to connect certain times of the day, month, or year with various activities and their associated meanings. We often set up rituals surrounding times of transition, such as waking, going to bed, eating meals, birthdays, holidays, or celebrations with others.

As you color in this image, drawn from the royal palace in Thailand, consider your own personal set of rituals. What do they surround? Are they healthy and do they serve you well? Would you like to discard any as outdated or ill-fitting?

Open your mind to possibilities for creating new rituals for yourself that work to support the best of who you are.

This image depicts a floating village on the Mekong River in Cambodia. All of the houses, stores, means of transportation and even schools exist on the water. How mind-expanding to imagine this sort of lifestyle! While it is familiar and even easy to get along with people just like us, an important aspect of open-mindedness means embracing cultural differences with interest and without fear or judgment.

As you complete this drawing, please consider where you feel open to people of different cultures, classes, and sexual orientations, and where you have trouble remaining open. What would it take to open your heart and mind more fully? How can you increase their own empathy for those with whom you feel less open? After you complete this drawing, please consider creating your own image to facilitate this process.

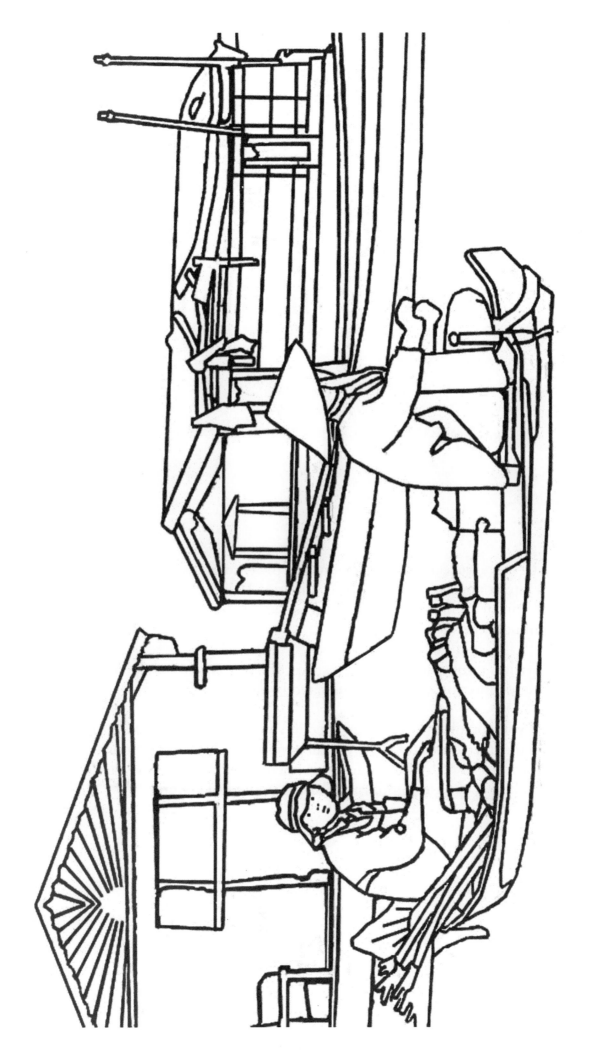

Interconnection

The more we learn about the universe, the clearer it is that everything is interconnected. No person is an island. All living creatures enjoy a continual exchange of matter, energy, and information across open boundaries.

Mystics throughout the ages strive for a spiritual awakening to interconnection, such as is illustrated by this Chinese panel.

As you complete this drawing, see if you can achieve a direct sense of the interconnection between all people and things in the universe. The more directly you can feel this open-hearted stance, the easier it will be to cultivate compassion for all people and cultures.

CHAPTER FOUR
Enhancing Play and Creativity by Making Associations

An associative mind is an active quality of attention that jumps nimbly from one idea or image to another. We need an associative mind to solve problems, play with creative thoughts, and find novel solutions. Like an open mind, an associative mind shares the quality of receptivity. Yet, by tapping into the inner eyes, ears, and other senses of imagination, an associative mind simultaneously maintains direction and focus. When employing an associative mind, we avoid thinking in straight lines or using sequential logic to search for the right answer or a single truth. Instead, an associative mind moves in many directions at once in search of multiple solutions to challenges, such as "How many uses can you find for a nail?" In order to cultivate an associative quality of attention, we must relax effortful striving in order to sink into our interior world and tap the depths of the unconscious. By making this kind of inward journey, we cultivate nimble and flexible attention from the bottom up, through intuitive promptings, rather than operating from the top down, through consciously-directed thought. An associative mind is ideal whenever we wish to face complex problems or engage in creative enterprises.

When approaching the drawings in this module, please contemplate and practice your capacity for cultivating play and creativity through an associative mind. After collecting your materials, sharpening your pencils, and finding the right spot in which to draw, here is a guided meditation(adapted from Marks-Tarlow, 2014) to tap into this quality of mind:

Close your eyes. Take a few deep breaths to clear everything away. Then imagine that you are about to visit the Theater of the Soul. This is a venue grounded deep within each of us, a place in the imagination that contains all of the inner emotional truths that lie at the heart of the subjectivity of each one of us. Imagine that you wish to visit the Theater of the Soul in order to see a play or movie called "Welcome to Your Life." First, allow yourself to visualize the route to the theater. Open up each of your inner senses in order to perceive how you will get to the theater. What neighborhoods do you travel through? What do the streets look like? How about the houses? Is it an urban or rural environment? How are you dressed? Are you alone or with someone? When you reach the theater, what does the building look like? What size and style of architecture? Upon arriving at the front door, feel free to enter the theater, look around as much as you wish, until you feel ready to take your seat. Notice whether you are alone or with others in the audience. Check out the décor surrounding the stage. After you have taken in all the sights and sounds, imagine that the theater lights start to dim. Now, sit back and enjoy as the action begins, whether in the form of a dramatic stage production or movie. Try not to anticipate the action or actors. Instead, simply watch. As you do so, take careful note not only of what you see, but also of how you feel as you watch. After the production has finished, allow yourself to remain seated for a moment. You may wish to close the inner eyes of your imagination in order to reflect on what you just witnessed. Then whenever you are ready, open your inner eyes as well as your outer eyes and return to the room, knowing you can return to this theater any time you wish.

Inner Maps

Each of us inevitably seeks outer guidance—from friends, family, teachers and trusted others. Yet, in the end, it is the internal guidance of our intuition and inner counsel that provides the final say. We know ourselves best. Only we know how it feels to be us, which includes the full picture of our histories, experiences, strengths, and weaknesses. Unless we suffer from a devastating mental or physical condition, we are in the best position to put all the pieces together for ourselves. To learn to trust your intuitive foundations is true empowerment, from the inside out. This image maps the inner terrain of flashes, hunches, gut feelings, and other realms of intuition.

As you complete this drawing, please fill in your own words or icons in the various blank areas. Be sure to consider where on the map you are most and least comfortable standing. Which areas would you like to strengthen?

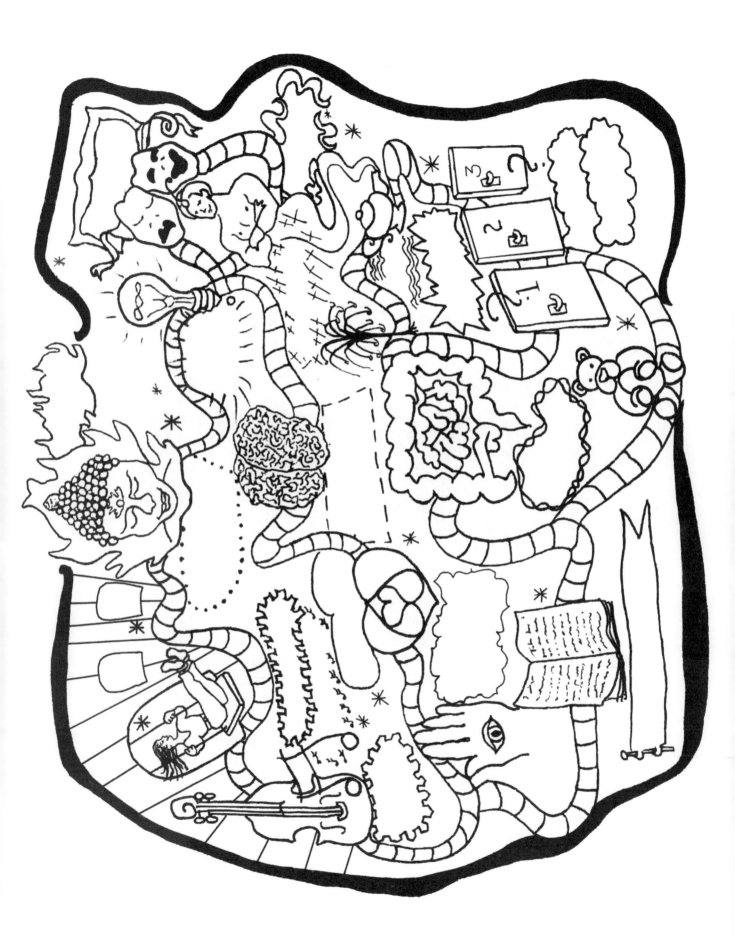

Personas are an important aspect of an associative mind. A persona is the social mask, or image, that we present to others or to the world at large. We develop personas in response to relationships we have and people we meet. Different cultures cultivate different personas. Some cultures value authenticity over social masks. Regardless, it is healthy to have a wide range of personas, which helps us to be socially flexible and situationally adaptable. At the same time, it is not so healthy to change who we appear to be so completely in response to other people and their needs that we become entirely chameleon-like, without an inner core.

As you fill in this African mask, consider your own range of personas. How much is dictated by family, culture or your peer group? How much is dictated by you? How healthy versus unhealthy does your range feel? Are there any changes you would like to make to the personas you present?

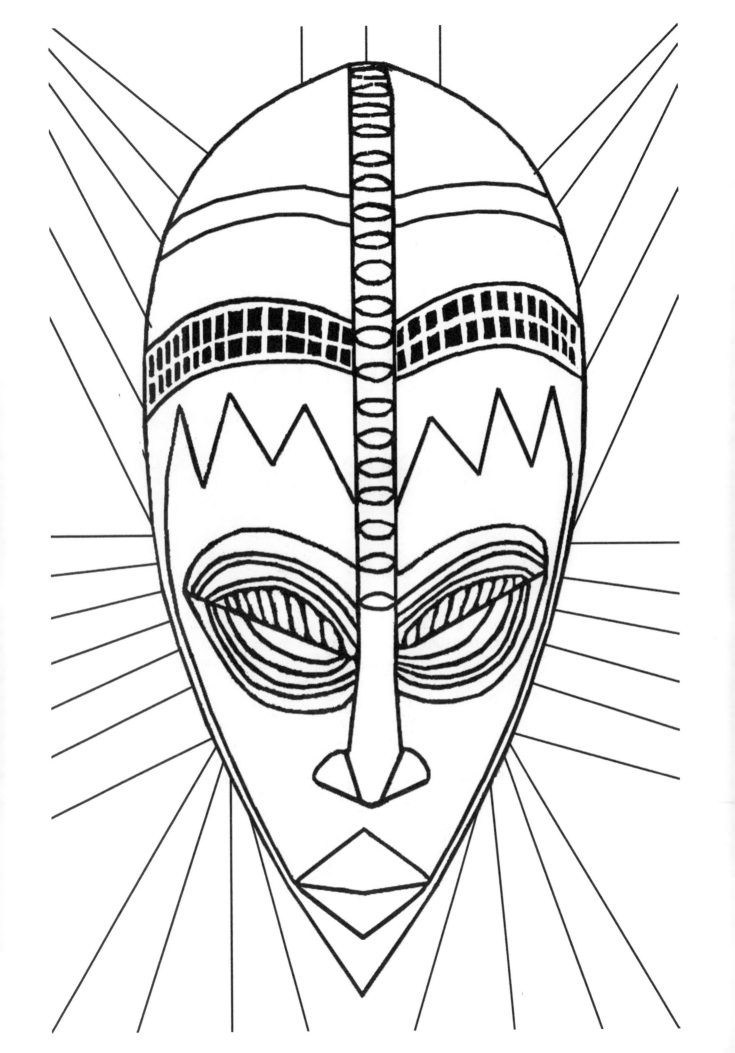

The essence of an associative mind is the ability to detect and create patterns. Our brains are inherent pattern-makers. How often have you noticed whales, elephants or witches in the random contours of fluffy clouds? Scientists detect patterns in nature, while artists design patterns of their own making. We understand one another and ourselves by detecting patterns in behavior. We make meaning in life by finding patterns in the unique combination of genes, upbringing and chance that represent the sum total of our lives.

As you complete this drawing, please contemplate the kinds of patterns you habitually notice. In your own life, which patterns are you attracted to? Do they serve you well? Are there other sorts of patterns you would prefer to notice? How can you increase your ability to do so?

Our most creative impulses emerge from unknown origins deep within the unconscious. To open ourselves to the farthest reaches of the associative mind, we must allow ourselves to be surprised. The more we expect and can predict what happens next, both in inner or outer worlds, the more we are in touch with our analytic, rather than associative side of mind.

There is a shaggy dog story about a man absolutely sick of the repetitive repartee. He goes through extraordinary and expensive lengths so that when his partner returns home and predictably asks, "What's new?" he unpredictably answers, "There's a dead horse in the bathtub!" Surprise!

We all need safe surprises to spark wonder and stretch our minds. This drawing contributes by reversing observed with observer. The baby who should be outside the jack-in-the-box is inside instead. Add your own designs to the walls and floor. Contemplate the role of surprise in your life—both as giver and receiver.

Totems

This Tlinget bear carving represents a totem of the peoples of the far north of America. Many cultural patterns involve animal totems, or guides. This especially holds for traditional and indigenous peoples.

As you fill in this page, let your mind wander freely. Which animal resonates most deeply with your innermost self as guide? Relax into feeling rather than thinking your way towards an answer. Let your imagination play with whatever animal you choose. Is there an adventure to be had together? What wisdom or guidance is available from your animal guide?

Free Play

Along with the safety and understanding of a responsive caregiver during early and middle childhood, nothing is more important than free play. Pretend scenarios represent the associative mind at its highest. As children try on different roles, they develop new connections and learn how to internalize society's rules. By stretching emotional, social, behavioral and cognitive aspects, the early free play of imagination sets the stage for vision and creativity throughout life.

Before coloring these children at play, create your own backdrop. As you draw, reflect upon the kinds of pretend games you used to play as a child. Can you see connections between how you played then and who you are now? How do you play today? Do you play enough to rejuvenate and inspire you? What, if anything, would you like to alter about how you play?

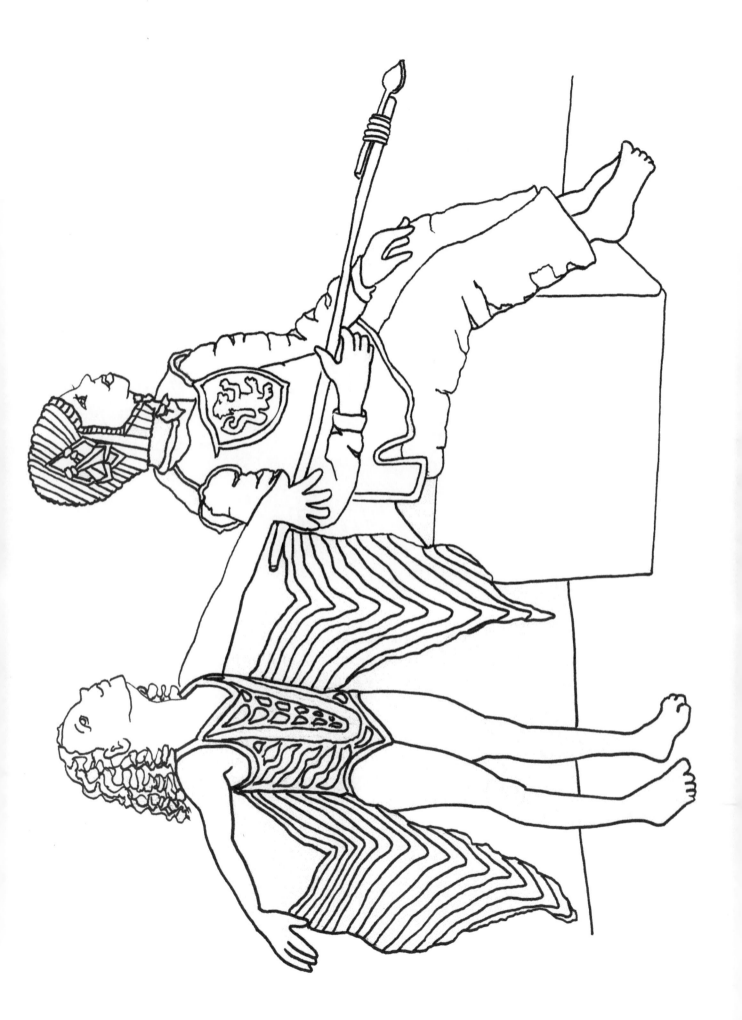

Glee!

The girl in this image opens her body to the glee of being high on Jack's beanstalk. Little inspires us more than allowing magic seeds to take root in our imagination, so that they may sprout and grow and transport us to fantasy lands where anything can happen.

As you complete this drawing, contemplate your own capacity for imaginative glee. How does it arise? When was the last time your body felt as open as the girl's in this image? Is there something you need to add to your life to open yourself up to more glee?

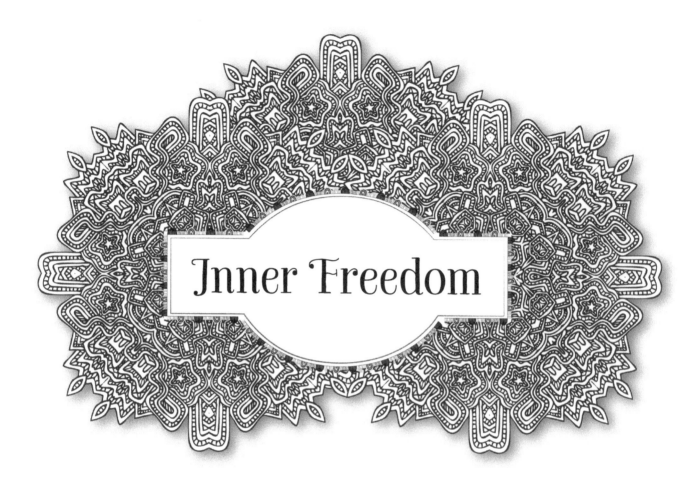

Inner Freedom

Viktor Frankl reputedly said, "Between stimulus and response there is a space. In that space is our power to choose our response. In our response lie our growth and our freedom." Frankl's associative mind was so strong that he found meaning even while imprisoned in a Nazi concentration camp, where so many others around him were doomed to die.

The ability to find meaning in every aspect of experience is the greatest freedom of associative mind.

As you complete this drawing, muse on your own sense of inner freedom. How do you make meaning? Are you a victim or a free agent within your inner narratives? Can you find meaning in everything that happens, including negative or unwanted events? If something blocks your capacity here, what is it? How can you expand your sense of inner space and freedom?

Just as we each have a shadow side, we also have the capacity for dark play. This might involve fantasies—whether sexual or not—of pleasure or satisfaction in hurting others or being hurt ourselves. Dark play often represents attempts of our associative mind to deal with emotional trauma by repeating, compensating for or reversing past hurts. Such play is harmless, *if* the line between fantasy and reality is clear, everything is consensual, and everybody remains safe. Also, it is important that obsessional thoughts or activities don't fully colonize your mind or body.

As you fill in this drawing, contemplate your own darkest fantasies. How do you hold them? Do you understand their origins? Can you accept them without judgment or shame? What can they tell you about your emotional needs?

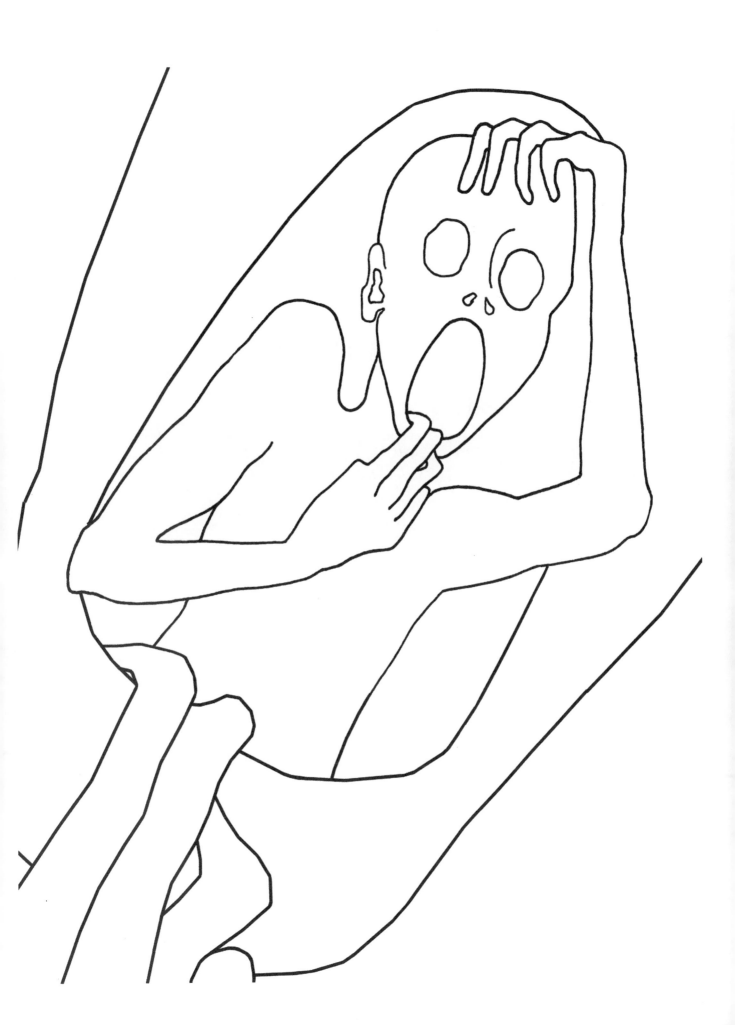

Why do children so love to wear masks at Halloween, while adults adore masquerade balls and dressing up for Mardi Gras? When we adopt various costumes, we play with different aspects of identity in a way that expands personal and social horizons.

As you complete this page, imagine what it would be like to wear each mask. Where might you wear it? What might happen inside it? Which mask, if any, might you choose to wear in real life? Why? If not one of these, can you create a mask for yourself in your mind or even draw it on a separate page if you dare?

The king's jester was an important figure who brought humor to the court, as well as the capacity to turn the order of things upside down. Psychologist Arthur Koestler considered humor the third pillar of creativity alongside art and science. We can't help but laugh when we experience a new and unexpected association. Meanwhile, an entire branch of yoga has arisen around the healing power of a deep belly laugh.

As you color in this drawing, pay mindful attention to the role of humor in your life. What makes you laugh? How often do you enjoy a deep belly laugh? Is it important to surround yourself with funny people? Do you express wit in conversation with others? Do you seek enough comedy in your free time?

Imagination

"It will happen when pigs fly" is an old expression referring to seemingly impossible events that actually come to pass. The power to bring positive and productive aspects of imagination into reality represents the associative mind at its finest. What seemed impossible yesterday—like flying machines or communicating instantly across the planet—is commonplace today. The germs of all new ideas and products sprouted from the ground of impossibility within someone's imagination.

Please add additional background for these flying pigs. As you complete the drawing, dare yourself to imagine something seemingly impossible that you could work to make happen.

CHAPTER FIVE

Fostering a Compassionate Mind to Take Care of Self and Others

People are inherently social. Collectively we may engage in war or "duke it out" in competition, yet individually, each of us requires nurturance, cooperation and support. We need love literally to survive as babies and emotionally to thrive during later stages of life. When we care deeply for others, we experience the desire to serve. And when we serve others—whether family, friends, or strangers—we are most likely to feel fulfilled. In fact, simply by practicing loving kindness meditation, we can stimulate positive emotions and raise our mood.

A compassionate mind enables us to work cooperatively with others and treat them with understanding and kindness. This stance becomes especially important whenever we encounter people with different values; people who come from different cultures; or people who possess different sexual orientations. Tibetan culture is especially interesting, because no distinction exists between compassion towards the self and compassion towards others. The two qualities of mind work hand-in-hand in a culture that experiences very little self-contempt or judgmental attitudes towards others.

When approaching the drawings in this module, please practice your capacity to care for self and others. After collecting your materials, sharpening your pencils, and finding the right spot in which to draw, here is a guided meditation to help open up a compassionate mind:

Close your eyes, take a couple of deep breaths, and begin by turning your focus to your chest area. Let yourself feel gratitude for your own heart, as it beats tirelessly moment after moment, day after day, to circulate oxygen throughout your body. Breathe in and out from that area, as if your breath, along with all of the rest of your emotion-filled experience is starting from your heart rather than your nose. As you continue to breathe in and out from your heart center, let yourself visualize and imagine warmth, heat or even prickles of light in this area of your body. At the same time, allow yourself to direct corresponding feelings of kindness, consideration, and love toward yourself. Try to notice any self-criticism, judgment, numbness, or negative feelings that may block your experience of warmth, heat, or light. After acknowledging any blocks, let yourself drop beneath all of this in search of a place of self-caring. Here, you wish only the best for yourself. As you keep your focus on the warmth, heat, or light, repeat the following phrases to yourself several times, either silently or out loud:

> **May I be free from inner violence and outer harm;**
> **May I be free from mental pain and physical suffering;**
> **May I find happiness, joy, and ease in life, exactly as I am.**

After repeating this mantra several times, turn your attention to a person who you care about deeply. Repeat the same phrases now directed towards that individual, keeping your focus within your heart center. Next, choose an acquaintance or person you hardly know; direct these same heartfelt phrases towards that person. Then, select someone with whom you have conflict or difficult feelings; repeat these same phrases to the best of your ability. Finally, imagine the lovingkindness warmth, heat, and light of your heart center radiating out to all sentient beings, including yourself.

Safety must be had before compassion can be cultivated. Babies in the womb are automatically connected and protected at every level—body, mind, brain. Everything mother eats, every way she moves, even how she feels is part of a growth-promoting environment. Nature automatically creates a compassionate container for new life.

As you complete this drawing, pay mindful attention to that which enhances your own physical, emotional, and spiritual safety. Do you have what you need in this area? If not, how can you increase your sense of safety in the world?

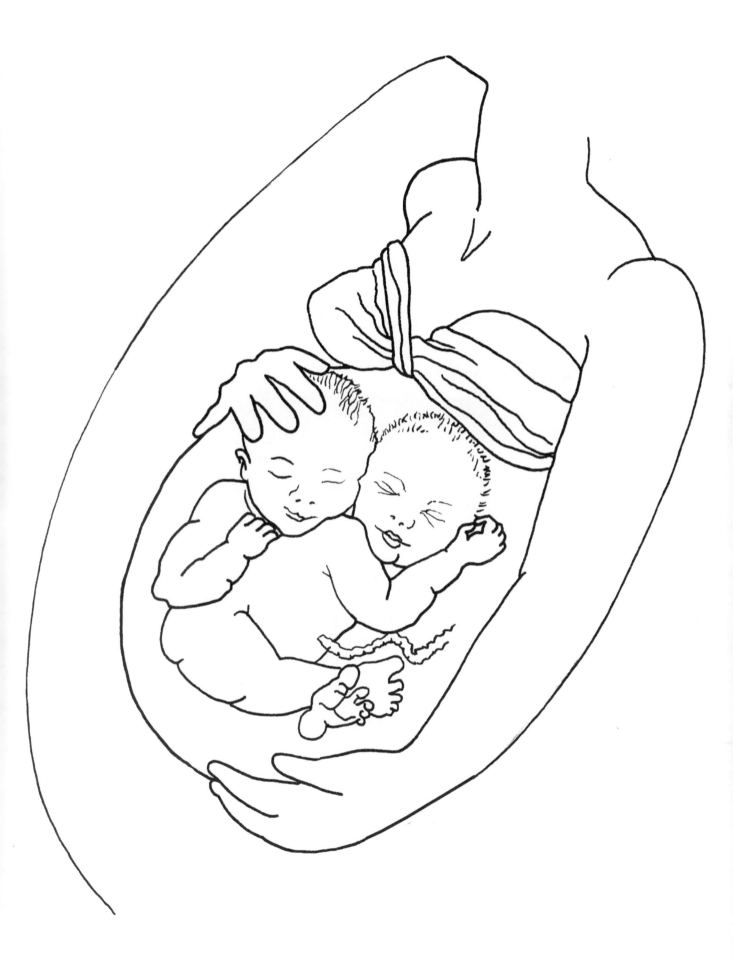

Attachment

From the moment of birth, how we feel, think, and even perceive the world itself is shaped by the quality of care we receive. If our caregivers are tuned into our feelings and needs and able to reflect our true selves back to us, then we grow up to feel relatively secure and trusting of people and circumstances.

As we grow, it becomes up to us to find people and activities to help calm and comfort ourselves. Petting animals and making art are both good ways to self-soothe. They quiet the mind, while the repetitive motion of our hands reminds us of being stroked.

As you draw, imagine the movements of your hand as a way to stroke and comfort your soul. Drawing is an excellent way to self-soothe through its rhythmic motions. The more actively you set the intention to relax and calm yourself through drawing, the more effective the process will be.

Self-Care

In airplanes throughout the world a safety card exists, much like this drawing. The message is clear: we can only help others once we have secured our own safety and care. This is true across the board, physically, emotionally, and spiritually. The better we take care of ourselves, the more available we can be to others.

As you complete this drawing, consider the quality of your self-care and how you might enhance it. Keep in mind that true self-care often involves discipline, that self-care differs from self-indulgence, and that taking care of ourselves isn't always fun.

Remember to give yourself credit for enhancing your well-being with this book!

Affection

While our work and professional lives are important, it is the quality of our relationships, including friendships, that determines the quality of our lives. No matter what we are doing, it is always a good idea to take the time to slow down, hang out with others, and "smell the roses." Putting energy into our friendships is a crucial form of self-care.

As you complete this drawing, consider the quality of your friendships. Picture each of your close friends, one at a time, and direct some lovingkindness his or her way. If you don't have enough friends, imagine making some new ones, then send lovingkindness in their direction. Finally, envision yourself to direct a random act of kindness towards a stranger.

Children are the world's most precious resource. Each generation tends to the world's garden, and it is up to us to tend to our children as the next generation of gardeners. The more we invest in our children, the more they can invest in the world.

As you complete this drawing, contemplate how you relate to the children in your life. Imagine taking a little extra time to help them feel seen and special. If there aren't any children in your life, imagine relating to a young child who is a stranger. Alternatively, dream about tending to your own inner child or a child you might like to have one day in the future.

Respect is an important sign of caring and compassion in Japanese culture, which preserves social harmony. Whatever our culture, we each convey respect through how we use language, how we use our body to attend to others, plus subtle forms of non-verbal communication by which emotion and intention get expressed.

In any culture, self-respect is equally important as respect for others. We feel best about ourselves when we act according to our own values and principles. This stance includes self-forgiveness for our short-comings.

As you complete this drawing, contemplate the quality of your respect for others and for yourself. Are you in balance between these two directions? If not, how might you address any imbalances?

It is relatively easy to show compassion for people in our own social groups, especially when they look much like us. It is more difficult to express care for people whose features, culture, religion, language, or customs bear little resemblance to our own. The challenge heightens the more we are bombarded by local and world news that piques fears and fuels anger. Yet, if we are ever to achieve peace on this planet, this is the most essential practice of all.

As you complete this drawing, consider your capacity to extend compassion and care to people you define as Other than you. If you notice any blocks, consider what they are and whether you are willing and able to soften them. Make your own drawing to represent social harmony and world peace.

The essence of compassion involves love. Of course, personal love for our partners, family members, and close friends differs from a more dispassionate love for co-workers, strangers, or humankind as a whole. In all cases, however, when we shine with love, we give ourselves and others a gift that is infectious.

Feel free to add faces and more background to this drawing. As you complete this page, work from your heart area. Let it open and shine as you contemplate the quality of the love you hold for others.

Far Eastern Indian culture has some of the most elaborate rituals for marriage. A traditional wedding ceremony lasts three days. Intricate henna patterns may be drawn on the hands and feet of the bride and other female guests. The groom often arrives to the ceremony on a white horse, or even an elephant. In contemporary culture, the institution of marriage is expanding to include same sex couples. Whether in traditional or nontraditional form, the art of showing care and compassion for our most intimate mate is the foundation for a healthy family. We easily look to our spouses for love and care. What is harder is to keep our focus on the love and care we have to offer them.

As you complete this drawing, contemplate your capacity to provide love and care, either in the marriage you are in or in the one you dream of someday. Imagine extending love not only in response to positive, admirable traits of your partner, but also in response to his or her blind spots, faults, and shortcomings.

As we face life's uncertainties, wage peace with our shadow sides, risk crossing life's thresholds, and navigate the mazes set before us, we are often rewarded by wisdom. Life is all too often filled with pain, suffering and hardship. But wisdom is the consolation prize that feeds the soul.

As you complete this drawing, see if you can access the still and deep well of your own wise side. Bathe in its waters. Have compassion for your life's journey as a whole.

Western culture places great emphasis on becoming independent, yet this is not the fate of the world at large. As most of us live further away from the land, and as society grows more complex, we become ever more dependent upon one another for food, clothes, shelter, entertainment—nearly everything in our lives.

When we recognize how much we lean on one another to make society work, it becomes much easier to adopt a stance of care and compassion for others.

As you complete this drawing, consider how much of your life is dictated by interdependence. What are you grateful for? What opportunities and things have been provided by others? Imagine the full chain of people it took simply to produce the shirt on your back. How can you cultivate a more active stance of gratitude in your daily life?

The more connected we feel to the Earth, the more we recognize that each action we take reverberates all the way through Mother Nature's vast web of interdependence. Once we open ourselves up to this level of unity, we can't help but want to tread mindfully to preserve the Earth's resources and splendors.

As you complete this drawing, please consider how green your footprint is. How do you feel about your own use of resources? Are you satisfied with your level of attentiveness? Are there any changes you would like to make to soften your step and help to preserve the world's resources?

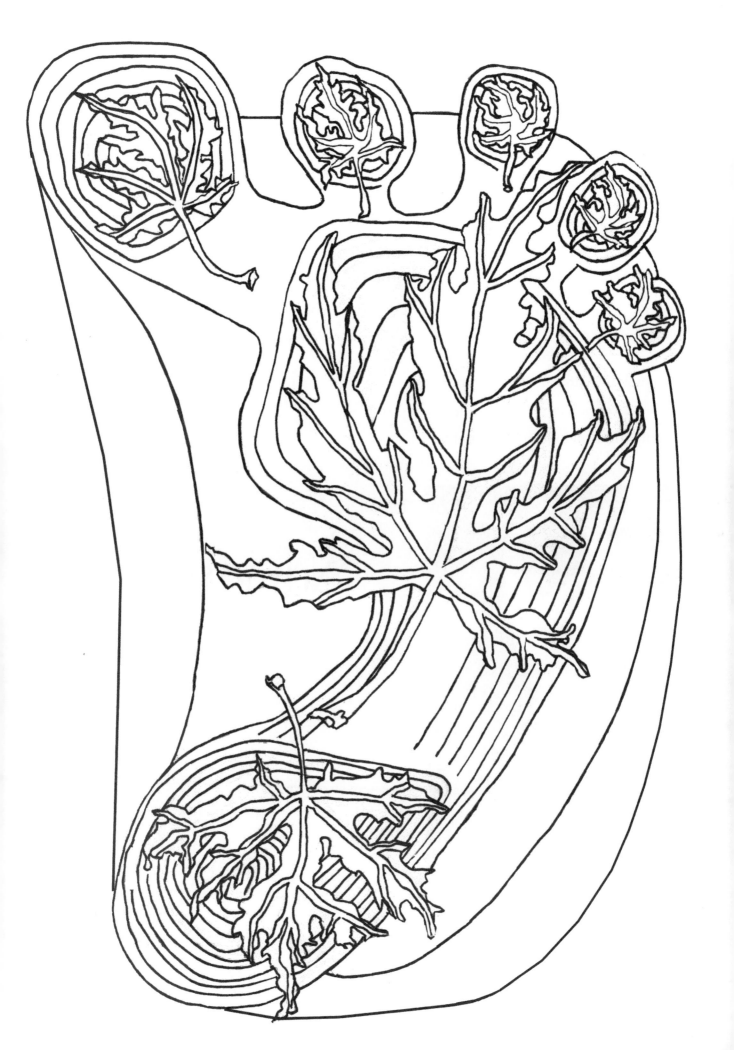

Additional Resources

Most of the guided meditations were adapted from *Awakening Clinical Intuition*.
Many of the images in this book were originally published as illustrations in the following books.

Marks-Tarlow, T. (2014). *Awakening Clinical Intuition: An Experiential Workbook for Psychotherapists.*
New York: WW Norton.

Marks-Tarlow, T. (2012). *Clinical Intuition in Psychotherapy: The Neurobiology of Embodied Response.*
New York: WW Norton.

Marks-Tarlow, T. (2008). *Psyche's Veil: Psychotherapy, Fractals and Complexity.* New York: Routledge.

www.TrulyMindfulColoring.com

www.facebook.com/TrulyMindfulColoring

TrulyMindfulColoring@hotmail.com

Namaste!